GET OUT OF DEBT!

Smart Solutions to Your Money Problems

Steve Rhode & Mike Kidwell

PUBLISHED BY
DEBT COUNSELORS OF AMERICA®

Get Out Of Debt! Smart Solutions to Your Money Problems
First Edition
By Steve Rhode & Mike Kidwell

Cover and Book Design by Kieran Daly
Photography by Doug Sanford
Cartoons by Ted Goff

This compilation
©1999 Debt Counselors of America, Incorprated.

This book is intended to provide accurate information to educate you about the financial issues we encounter the most. This book is not intended to be a substitute for legal, investment, or financial planning advice. If you need legal or financial planning advice, you should consult with a lawyer, investment advisor, financial planner, or other professional in your state.

All rights reserved. No part of this publication may be reproduced or transmitted in any form or by any means, electronic or mechanical, including photocopying, facsimile, recording, or by any information or retrieval system without permission in writing from the Author and Publisher, except for the inclusion of brief quotations in a review.

Debt Counselors of America®
1680 East Gude Drive
Rockville, MD 20850
Phone: (301) 762-5270
www.GetOutOfDebt.org

Debt Counselors of America®, DCA®, Debt Counselors®, and One-Pay® are registered service marks of Debt Counselors of America, Inc. Crisis Relief Team^{sm}, CRT^{sm}, Get Out Of Debt^{sm} - The Radio Show, and On-Track^{sm} are servicemarks of Debt Counselors of America, Inc.

Printed in The United States of America. First printing: September, 1999

Library of Congress Catalog Card Number: 99-65925

ISBN 0-9670255-0-8

This book is dedicated to our families,
Pam and Mandy Rhode and Gina Kidwell.

Without your support and understanding we would never have been able achieve our dream of being able to help people get out of debt. Thank you for letting us spend the days together helping others. We will never forget what you have sacrificed for us.
We will love you always.

A special dedication goes to Teresa Siemers.
Without her special help and assistance, none of what we have been able to accomplish would have been possible.
We'll miss you forever.

ACKNOWLEDGMENTS

No great feat is ever accomplished alone. That is certainly true for this text. It represents the work of many people over the past couple of years, great people like Gerri Detweiler and Robin Leonard. Gerri and Robin are two of the most knowledgeable personal finance experts around today. Their depth of knowledge and compassion for helping others is unmatched.

We also have the privilege of working daily with staff members who have dedicated their skills and personality to this book. Kieran Daly has cheerfully tackled the design, layout and production of this book. Bussie Parker has spent countless hours making sure all of the written words enjoy being next to one another. Judy Branzelle and Wayne Ruckman have also made significant contributions. Cindy Stark has been an endless source of energy and an inspiration to the team. And to Jonathan Adkins and Tina Payne-Smallwood, thank you for all of your assistance.

Finally, without the support and understanding of the greatest staff of people in the world at Debt Counselors of America® we never would have been able to complete this book. If it wasn't for the teamwork and compassion that we all feel at Debt Counselors®, we never would have never achieved even one tenth of what we have. We are truly blessed by your support, help, friendship, and the belief that together we can make a difference in people's lives.

Steve Rhode and Mike Kidwell
Rockville, Maryland

Table of Contents

INTRODUCTION

DEALING WITH DEBT

CHAPTER 1	The 20 Greatest Myths About Credit and Debt	1
CHAPTER 2	Five Easy Ways to Get Out of Debt	7
CHAPTER 3	Drowning in Student Loans?	11
CHAPTER 4	What to Do When the Debt Collector Calls	17
CHAPTER 5	Forgotten Regulations That You Can Use to Make Your Creditors Treat You Fairly	23
CHAPTER 6	Beware of the IRS if You Settle or Default on a Debt	29

CREDIT

CHAPTER 7	Nine Ways to Improve Your Credit Profile	33
CHAPTER 8	Ten Ways to Repair Your Credit	37
CHAPTER 9	How to Use the New Credit Reporting Law to Help You Get and Keep Good Credit	45
CHAPTER 10	Credit Scoring: How It Works and Actions You Can Take to Improve Your Score and Get Approved for Credit	51
CHAPTER 11	How to Get All the Cheap Credit You Want	57
CHAPTER 12	Plastic Power: Strategies for Making the Most of Your Credit Cards	61
CHAPTER 13	Credit Card or Debit Card: The Great Debate	65

MORTGAGES AND CAR LOANS

CHAPTER 14	Should You Lease Your Next Vehicle?	73
CHAPTER 15	How to Buy a Car With Marks on Your Credit	83
CHAPTER 16	When You Can't Make Your Car Payments	89
CHAPTER 17	Repossession... Why It Happens, What You Can Do, and Your Rights Before, During and After	93
CHAPTER 18	How to Buy a House With Marks on Your Credit	103
CHAPTER 19	What to Do When You Can't Pay the Mortgage	109

BANKRUPTCY AND DIVORCE

CHAPTER 20	Bankruptcy: Is It Right for Me?	115
CHAPTER 21	What to Do to Never File Bankruptcy Again	121
CHAPTER 22	Making a Clean Financial Break at Divorce	127

CONTRACTS AND LEGAL ISSUES

CHAPTER 23	What to Do if You Are Sued	133
CHAPTER 24	Stuck in a Contract: What to Do Before and After You Sign Up for Clubs (Health/Timeshare/Camping/Travel)	139
CHAPTER 25	Child Support: Answers to Commonly Asked Questions	147
CHAPTER 26	Bounced Checks: What to Do if You Write Them or Receive Them	153

SPECIAL CONSIDERATION FOR THE MILITARY

CHAPTER 27	How Being in Debt Can Affect Your Military Career	159
CHAPTER 28	How the Soldiers' and Sailors' Civil Relief Act Can Help You	163

TIPS FOR SUCCESS

CHAPTER 29	How to Cut Your Holiday Bills in Half Without Feeling Like a Scrooge	171
CHAPTER 30	How to Send Your Kids Back to School Without Breaking the Bank	175
CHAPTER 31	How to Use Credit Cards in College and Not Get In Over Your Head	179
CHAPTER 32	How to Be Financially Successful When You Graduate	183
CHAPTER 33	How to Come Back From Vacation With Money in Your Pocket	193
CHAPTER 34	How to Start Your Own Successful Business With Little Money	199
CHAPTER 35	Identity Theft: How to Protect Yourself and What to Do if You Are a Victim	205

INDEX   **213**

INTRODUCTION

When we started Debt Counselors of America®, it was because we wanted to help people get out of debt. As we worked with more and more consumers, we found that people needed help with more than past due bills. We received countless e-mails from people who were dealing with other serious financial issues:

My car was repossessed. What are my rights?

I can't afford to pay my mortgage. What do I do?

My situation seems hopeless. Is bankruptcy my only option?

We started to answer the most common questions posed to us in a series of self-help publications which we made available through the Debt Counselors of America website. Before we knew it, we had developed an extensive library of resources to help people deal with a number of specific money issues. We present the best of that library here in this book.

Throughout these pages, you will discover some basic truths about handling money, and you'll learn about your rights should you run into difficulty. We hope you will use these chapters to build better spending habits, to become a more informed consumer, and to learn how to take control of your finances. When you take control of your finances, you take control of your future.

CHAPTER 1

The 20 Greatest Myths About Credit and Debt

MYTH 1: My financial condition is so bad that my situation is hopeless.

REALITY: Although your problem may not be solved in a way that you would envision, a resolution can always be found. Open your mind and be realistic about your options. Ultimately, you have to choose a solution with which you are most comfortable.

MYTH 2: If I co-sign on a loan, the lender will never come after me.

REALITY: Wrong. You co-signed for the loan, which means you promised to repay the debt if the borrower couldn't. When the borrower is unable to pay back the loan, you are on the hook. Unless you are prepared to repay the loan when the borrower defaults, you should never co-sign any loan.

MYTH 3: If I don't use credit, I'll never have anything.

REALITY: If you don't use credit, you won't have debt. Remember when people used to pay for purchases in cash? If you want something bad enough, save for it. It is significantly more rewarding to purchase something and own it outright than creating another liability that you owe.

MYTH 4: Credit is bad.

REALITY: Wrong. Credit can be used for many good and worthwhile purposes, such as buying a home. Credit cards are very convenient when making purchases as long as you've got the money to pay off the credit card bill. (See Chapter 12, "Plastic Power..." to see how you can use credit to your advantage.) Credit is like many other things in life: when used incorrectly, it can hurt you.

MYTH 5: I can solve all of my financial problems if I sign up for this fantastic work-at-home business opportunity I heard about.

REALITY: Possibly. However, most people invest their last few dollars into such an opportunity, hoping it will save them from financial misfortune. They usually don't have enough business experience to be immediately successful, and once they invest their available funds getting into the program, they don't have enough money to sufficiently operate the business. Don't believe that you will be rich just because the person that told you about the opportunity appears to be doing well. That person probably has much larger bills than you do, and is trying to recruit as many people as possible into the program to keep himself from sinking.

If you have extra money to play with, then get involved and have a good time. But be prepared to lose both the time and money you invested. Do it because it's fun and you really enjoy the people you work with, not because you are betting that the business will solve your problems.

MYTH 6: I must get out of financial trouble with zero negative marks on my credit history.

REALITY: Some people would sell their souls to have a stellar credit report. Why? If they have a negative mark on their credit report, would that prevent them from getting more unsecured credit? Maybe. Would that be so bad? Isn't that how they got themselves into trouble in the first place?

Having a negative mark on your credit report does not mean you won't be able to get credit. It won't stop you from buying a house or car. Often, the most important factor in buying a home or car is not how spotless your credit is, but how much of a down payment you put down. Having a negative mark also does not mean you won't be able to get a credit card. You can get a secured credit card, where you put down a deposit. There is less risk to the lender since he has the security of the deposit, and therefore, he is more lenient in his lending guidelines.

Many people who are always worried about their spotless credit records do something dangerous, such as taking out a home equity loan that they can't afford to cover their debt payments, or taking a cash advance on their credit card(s) to make their monthly payments. All of this borrowing for what? Just so they won't have a negative mark on their credit report? If you're having a tough time, then do the best you can. If you fall a little behind, it's possible you might have some problems with lenders in the future. However, you may send a 100-word statement to the credit bureau(s) explaining your situation. The statement will appear on your credit report, enabling future creditors to understand what happened to you and why you temporarily fell behind.

MYTH 7: I'm a loser and a failure because I'm in financial trouble.

REALITY: You have to accept responsibility for your actions and remember that you did accept the credit with the promise of paying it back. But most families and our schools do a poor job of teaching financial responsibility. How many classes did you take while growing up that taught you how much credit you should accept? Maybe the truth is that you did make a mistake and you got in over your head because you didn't know better. If you can learn from this mistake, you are neither a loser nor a failure. Accept your setback, learn from it, and move on.

MYTH 8: My credit card company is taking advantage of me by charging 22% interest.

REALITY: Were you forced to get a credit card from that particular bank? If you were unaware of the interest rate before you completed the application, you should have inquired. By using the card, you accepted the bank terms, no matter what they were. If you don't want to be charged a high interest rate, either don't get the card or, when the bill comes, pay the entire balance within the grace period.

MYTH 9: My lender wouldn't have approved the loan if I couldn't afford it.

REALITY: Wrong. Some lenders are paid bonuses for lending you money up to and beyond your ability to repay. Ultimately, you are the only one to ensure that you do not get in over your head.

MYTH 10: If my debts get to be too much, I'll just file bankruptcy.

REALITY: Bankruptcy is a very serious matter and should be a last resort, not an easy "out." It is a legal case filed with the bankruptcy court that is a matter of public record, and it can be reported for the rest of your life if you apply for certain loans, life insurance, or jobs. Many people who filed bankruptcy wish they had tried other alternatives before filing. Once you file, you will always be "a person that filed bankruptcy," and you can never take that back. Take a look at Chapters 20 and 21 for more information on bankruptcy.

MYTH 11: The credit card companies wouldn't send me applications in the mail if I couldn't afford it.

REALITY: Wrong. The credit card companies are simply making you an offer based on mailing lists or research they have performed. It is your responsibility to determine if you can afford to accept their offer.

MYTH 12: Since I have no assets, the creditors can't do anything if I don't pay my bills.

REALITY: If you don't pay your bills, creditors may sue you, obtain a judgment against you, then enforce that judgment by garnishing your wages or waiting until you have assets. Chances are that you won't be broke forever, and creditors will wait for that day (while their interest is building). Although collection activity might currently be quiet, your account will most likely be sold to another agency and the collection calls will start again.

MYTH 13: Somewhere, there is a magic solution to my money problems.

REALITY: Wrong. Sometimes, you really do run out of good options, and you'll have to choose between unpopular solutions. Unlike television or the movies, there is not always a happy ending.

MYTH 14: Everything is okay because I pay the minimum payment due each month.

REALITY: By just paying the minimum payment on a debt, you extend your payments for many years. If possible, send more than the minimum payment. If this isn't possible, you are probably living close to the financial edge. What would happen if you were injured or sick and could not work? Would you be able to pay your bills if your spouse was suddenly out of work, or your company downsized and released you? Do you have any assets or cash reserves that you could fall back on? Simply being able to live from paycheck to paycheck is not a sign of financial well-being. Look at Debt Counselors of America's® Debt Eliminator[SM] report at www.GetOutOfDebt.org to design a personal plan for getting yourself out of debt as quickly as possible.

MYTH 15: People that look wealthy are wealthy.

REALITY: People that look wealthy often have big bills that they can't afford. They might be living in a fancy house and driving a fancy car, but sleeping on lawn chairs and avoiding the repo man.

MYTH 16: I'll never have money to retire.

REALITY: With that attitude you probably won't. Most people simply give up because it is more fun to spend money than it is to save it. However, you can build a fortune starting with just a few dollars. The keys to financial success are continuity and time; the earlier you begin to invest, the more you will have when you retire. Don't be concerned about where you are going to invest your money when you begin. Just start with a simple savings account. It doesn't pay much in interest, but you can develop the habit of regularly investing your money (at least monthly) while you look around and decide where you want to invest the funds for the long haul. You can invest in mutual funds, individual stocks, treasury bills, bond funds or a host of other investment vehicles. Go to the public library, bookstore or visit the Debt Counselors of America online bookstore at http://www.dca.org/bookstore.htm for good, easy to understand books on investing your money.

MYTH 17: All I need is for someone to give me a loan and that will solve my problems.

REALITY: Wake up. If you're having financial problems, a loan is usually a quick fix to a larger problem. By getting a loan, you are putting yourself deeper in debt just to make yourself believe that your problem is under control. Consolidation loans are often more costly over the long run, even though your monthly payment might be lower. You could end up consolidating no-interest debts like utilities and medical bills, and once consolidated, you'll end up paying interest. In addition, a consolidation loan usually requires you to put up some collateral, such as your home or vehicle, in the event that you default. Some consolidation loans can be beneficial. Make sure you have weighed the pros and cons before applying for a loan.

MYTH 18: It's wrong for my lender to take my collateral or sue me if I fall behind.

REALITY: When you signed the contract stating that if you failed to repay the loan, the lender could take the collateral or sue you, did you think the lender was kidding? Isn't that your signature on that contract?

MYTH 19: I can wrap up all of my credit card debt into a home equity loan and my interest will be tax deductible.

REALITY: You have just placed your home at risk and could lose it if you fail to make your payments. Nobody ever plans not to be able to make his payments. The reason the lender uses your home as collateral is so he can take it from you if you default on the loan. As for the tax deduction, who knows if the interest will be deductible for the life of the loan? Credit card interest used to be deductible but no longer is. Are you confident that home equity interest will always be deductible?

MYTH 20: It's okay if I take a cash advance to keep me from falling behind on my payments.

REALITY: Some people take cash advances on their credit cards to pay their other creditors "on time." It is better to accept a late payment than to borrow your way deeper into debt, just to pay for bills that you can't afford. What often happens is you put yourself so deep in debt that it is nearly impossible to improve your situation without significant negative marks being made on your credit report.

"There's nothing wrong with your personal finance software. You just don't have any money."

CHAPTER 2

Five Easy Ways to Get Out of Debt

"I can barely make my minimum payments each month."

"We can't seem to make our payments on time each month. We are always running late."

"I want something better for my family."

"We deserve to be happy but, with all of these debts, I can't see any light at the end of the tunnel."

"I wish my creditors would just leave me alone. I'll pay them when I'm able to."

Being in debt is both a financial condition and a state of mind.

As time passes, your state of mind can cross over into panic, anger, and eventually, depression. There is nothing redeeming about being knee-deep in debt, although certain types of debt, such as a home or car, are considered "good debt" by many.

To get out of debt, you need to reduce your available credit. This doesn't mean you'll be unable to do the things that you want to do. You can have those things you need to make your dreams come true. However, financial responsibility also means being able to achieve your goals without sacrificing your future for instant pleasure.

When you put yourself in debt, you are selling a part of your future for items/services you purchase today. You may have to take a job that you don't enjoy because you have entered yourself into a deal to swap future earnings for the dinner out, a new TV, a vacation, car, etc.

You're probably thinking you can't afford to pay for those things in cash, and you may be right. In your present situation, you're not in a financial condition that allows you to save up large amounts of cash, or even any at all. This is where you need to take control of your life.

STEP ONE:
Stop Incurring Debt

Sounds simple but it's not. Let's put aside your previous financial problems for a moment.

To stop a ship from sinking, you need to plug the leak. You first stop more water from coming in, and then worry about pumping it out. This same principal applies to getting out of debt. If you immediately stop doing the things that got you into debt, you won't put yourself further in debt. However, all of the fun things you were doing and buying were obtained on borrowed money. Ack! You've realized that you'll have to stop the "fun" stuff such as impulse buying, picking up the tab at dinner when out with friends, and buying more fun stuff. The process to change your spending behavior might be difficult.

To stop the slide into deeper levels of debt, you need to realize that your ultimate goal of being debt free is much more rewarding than the feeling you get when buying that new computer software or outfit. You cannot imagine the inner peace and satisfaction you will feel once financial freedom is achieved because you've never experienced it. But, being able to make your dreams come true is a wonderful feeling. To get to that place you must stop putting yourself further in debt. You must not spend one more dime for things you absolutely do not need. We aren't saying that you can't buy lunch out. We are saying that lunch out would be more satisfying if you did it just once a week, instead of every day. It would then become a treat instead of the norm. Pack your lunch four days a week and, if married, you will save about $160 a month.

STEP TWO:
Track the Cash

Do you know where you spend your money?

You can make guesses about how much you spend each month, but you're probably unaware of the actual amount. Before you can develop a game plan to achieve financial freedom, you need to identify your financial spending pattern. Everyone has his or her own pattern. To find yours, carry a pad and pen around with you.

Each time you spend money, write down the date, what it was for, and how much was spent. By simply writing down your expenses and reviewing the list, you will immediately cut out some of your unnecessary spending. This is usually a hard step for many to accomplish, so Debt Counselors of America® has developed the ON-TRACK® program to assist you (contact Debt Counselors of America at 1-800-680-3328).

At the end of the month you can break down your spending into categories such as: groceries, gas, rent/mortgage, etc. Then add up the individual items to find out exactly how much you spent in each area. Next, subtract the amount you spent during the month from the amount you earned. If you spent more than you earned you will need to either decrease your spending or increase your earnings. Review your previous month's spending and cut back in the areas where you are able if you are still having problems.

STEP THREE:
Plan for the Future

Before you begin to achieve financial success you first need to decide what your goals are.

Once you know the destination, you need to draw a map of how to get there. Write down your plan for becoming debt-free and read it often. You can revise it as many times as you'd like. Set goals that you are capable of achieving. Some good examples of goals are: spending less than you earn each month, making regular monthly deposits into a savings account, and cutting back on eating lunch out. As you begin to see that you are capable of achieving your financial goals, you will realize that you really can be debt-free.

STEP FOUR:
Instant Miracles

Don't expect instant miracles.

You didn't get into debt overnight and you're not going to get out of it overnight. Sudden debt is usually caused by accident, illness, or divorce. However, most people slip slowly into debt over a long period of time. Getting out of debt means changing spending habits that you learned since you were young. It's difficult, but it is possible. Be patient, stay on course, and enjoy your new rewards.

STEP FIVE: Seek Professional Help

Find someone who is financially wise, and ask him or her to help you achieve the same financial freedom he or she enjoys.

If you are unable to find someone that can help you, contact Debt Counselors of America for assistance.

CHAPTER 3

Drowning in Student Loans

If you can't make payments on your student loans, don't panic. Don't just give up and invite default, either. Default means that your credit will be damaged and your loan balance will increase dramatically with the addition of collection fees. And once you default, the holder of your loan will probably grab a portion of your paycheck and nab any tax refund to which you are entitled. If you're really unlucky, you'll be sued. Don't expect to be able to discharge your student loans in bankruptcy. As of October 7, 1998, all student loans are non-dischargeable in Chapters 7 and 13, except under the "undue hardship" provision, which is extremely difficult to show.

Fortunately, all student loan lenders offer a variety of repayment plans. So if you can't afford your current payments, don't assume that your current repayment plan is the only possible one. Consider all of the possible repayment options available to you.

Standard Repayment Plan

The original repayment scheme offered by your lender is known as a standard plan. With a standard plan, you usually pay the same amount each month for ten years. Standard repayment plans come with the highest monthly payments, but cost the least in the long run because the loans are paid off the quickest, meaning you pay less interest than you would pay with other repayment plans.

Graduated Repayment Plan

Under a graduated plan, your payments start out low and increase every few years. This is often the best option for people just starting a career or business who have a low income that's likely to increase steadily over time.

If you qualify for the graduated plan offered under the federal Direct Loan Program, your payments start at as little as half of what they would be under the standard plan, and then increase every few years. Other lenders' plans vary. Some require that you pay only the interest on your loans for a few years. Then you switch to payments of principal and interest until your loan is paid off. With any graduated repayment plan, you'll pay more for your loan over time than you would under a standard plan. Because interest charges are based on your unpaid balance each month, if you keep a higher balance in the early years of your loan, interest will add up quickly.

Extended Repayment Plan

Under an extended repayment plan, your payback term stretches over a period of 12 to 30 years, depending on your loan amount. Your fixed monthly payment is lower than it would be under the standard plan, but you'll pay more interest because the repayment period is longer. Most lenders let you combine the extended plan with graduated payments, which will lower your payments even further and increase your overall costs even more.

Income Contingent or Income Sensitive Repayment Plan

Under an income contingent or income sensitive repayment plan, each year your monthly payments are recalculated based on your prior year's annual income, household income and loan amount. The amount you pay annually will never exceed 20% of your discretionary income, that is, your annual gross income less an amount based on the poverty level for your household, as determined by the Department of Health and Human Services. To qualify for an income contingent plan, you must authorize the IRS to release your income information to the Department of Education.

If your income is very low, you may not be required to pay anything under an income contingent or income sensitive plan, or the amount you pay each month may be less than the amount of interest that is accumulating. This may feel like a relief, but be aware that as time goes on, your loan balance will continue to increase, and eventually it may seem as if you'll never get out from under.

If you're paying under a federal direct income contingent plan, the government will forgive any balance remaining on your loans after 25 years. Private lenders' income sensitive repayment plans contain no provision for loan forgiveness after 25 years.

Loan Consolidation

With loan consolidation, you can lower your monthly payments by combining several loans into one packaged loan and extending your repayment period. Most consolidation lenders won't accept your application unless you have an outstanding balance of at least $7,500 on your eligible loans. As with other low payment options, consolidating your loans will greatly increase the amount of interest you pay over the life of your loan. You may also be able to refinance several loans, or just one loan, to secure a lower interest rate. This is also called consolidation.

Many different lenders offer consolidation loans. Your repayment options will vary slightly depending on the lender you choose. For example, to consolidate under the federal Direct Loan Program (a very favorable program), you must either:

- have a federal direct student loan; or

- have tried and failed to obtain a consolidation loan with terms as good as those offered by the government.

All consolidation lenders allow you to stretch the term of your loan to anywhere from 12 to 30 years, depending on your balance. You can choose a fixed monthly payment for the life of the loan or a graduated payment plan.

If lengthening the repayment period doesn't bring down your monthly payment enough, you can choose a payment plan based on your income level. Income contingent and income sensitive plans are available for most consolidation loans.

Canceling Your Loans or Postponing Payments

If you've considered all repayment options and you still can't pay, all is not lost. In certain limited circumstances, you may be able to cancel your student loans. If you can't cancel your student loans, you can probably find a way to postpone making payments by obtaining a deferment or forbearance. A deferment is a delay based on a specific condition—such as returning to school or being unemployed—that excuses you from making payments for a set period of time. A forbearance is permission from your loan holder to stop making payments for a set period of time. Forbearances are easier to obtain than deferments because they are not tied to the type of loans you have or the date you obtained them, but they cost more. With a deferment, interest usually stops accruing. Not so with a forbearance. Here are the rules for cancellation and deferment:

- **Death of the borrower.** If a former student borrower dies, the executor can cancel any federal student loan.

- **Permanent total disability.** You can cancel any federal student loan if you are unable to work or go to school because of an injury or illness that is expected to continue indefinitely or result in your death.
- **Temporary total disability.** If you, your spouse or a dependent is temporarily totally disabled, you can defer the payments on most loans for up to three years.
- **Enrollment in rehabilitation program for the disabled.** If you are enrolled in a rehabilitation program for the disabled, you can defer payments on most loans.
- **Unemployment.** You can defer the payments on most loans, usually for up to three years if you are unemployed but looking for work.
- **Economic hardship.** You can defer payments on federal loans obtained after June 30, 1993 for up to three years if you are suffering an economic hardship. You are automatically entitled if you receive public assistance. Otherwise, qualifying is based on a mix of your income, the federal minimum wage, the federal poverty level and your monthly or annual federal student loan payments.
- **Parents with young children.** If you are a working mother or a mother or father on parental leave, you can often defer your student loan payments.
- **Enrollment in school.** If you return to school to study at least half-time, you can almost always defer the payments on your student loans.
- **Membership in a uniformed service.** If you currently serve the U.S. government in the U.S. military, the National Oceanic and Atmospheric Corps or the U.S. Public Health Service, there are several situations in which you may cancel or defer your loans.
- **Teaching needy populations.** If you teach certain needy populations, including low-income or disabled students, you may be able to have your student loans canceled or the payments deferred. You could get $5,000 of your student loans forgiven if you teach for five years in a low-income community.
- **Providing services other than teaching to needy populations.** If you serve certain needy populations (in a capacity other than teacher), you may be able to have your student loans canceled or payments deferred.
- **Performing community service.** In many situations, you can partially cancel your student loans or defer your payments in exchange for performing community service. Opportunities range from serving in the peace corps to volunteering your time with an organization that assists low-income people in your community.
- **Working as a healthcare professional.** If you are a healthcare professional, such as a nurse or a physician in your residency, you may qualify for loan cancellation or deferment.

- **Working in law enforcement.** Full-time law enforcement and corrections officers can cancel some older Perkins Loans.

- **Attended a trade school.** Many former students were lulled into taking out student loans to attend a trade school, only to have the school doors close before they could finish the program. Other students were falsely certified by school officials as being able to benefit from the loan. If this happened to you, you can probably cancel 100% of your federal student loan.

To apply for a new repayment plan, cancellation, deferment or forbearance, get in touch with the holder of your loan. If you are not in default, the holder of your loan is where you send your payments. And if the holder of your federal loans changes and you must send your payments to a different place, you must be notified within 45 days. If you are in default, the holder of your loan does not need to notify you when there is a change in where you must send your payments. If you don't know whom the holder of your loan is, contact either the Department of Education's Debt Collection Services Office at 800-621-3115 or the Federal Student Aid Information Center at 800-433-3243.

Options When You Have Defaulted on Your Student Loan

In the early 1990's, the student loan default rate skyrocketed. Lenders added so many extra charges when a loan went into default, such as collection costs and compounded interest, that many debtors stopped repaying their debts. In 1992, Congress passed laws allowing debtors who defaulted on their student loans to have a new chance to get their loan out of a default status. Since the new law was passed, the default rate has dropped significantly.

A loan generally defaults when payment has not been made for more than 180 days and no payment arrangements have been worked out with the lender. If you have a federal student loan, the most common way to get out of default is to request a reasonable and affordable repayment plan. Under this plan, the debtor asks the institution that holds the loan, such as a guarantee agency, the Department of Education or a collection agency, to allow payment that is reasonable and affordable. According to Robin Leonard, author of *Take Control of Your Student Loans*, published by Nolo Press, you should request a plan by saying one of the following:

- I want a reasonable and affordable repayment plan to renew my eligibility.
- I want to rehabilitate my loan.
- I want to qualify for loan consolidation.

Different lenders may use slightly different lingo but one of these should be understood by your lender.

The lender considers several factors in deciding what amount is reasonable and affordable for a particular debtor. These factors include the debtor's disposable income (how much money you are left with after deductions like Social Security, taxes, child support, etc.) and necessary expenses (food, housing, utilities, etc.). There are no formal rules specifying what amount is considered reasonable and affordable. Payment plans are designed to fit the particular situation of the debtor requesting it.

When requesting a plan, you want the lender to be sure to have an accurate picture of your finances. Therefore, you may want to attach copies of documents showing your expenses each month. Often, the agency will have a form on which you record and submit this information.

Within a few weeks, the lender will consider your request and will let you know the amount it expects you to pay each month. If you can't pay that amount, you should contact the lender immediately. You are only given one chance to get out of default. If you agree to make payments and then fail to pay, you probably will not have another opportunity to get out of default in this manner.

After you have made six consecutive on-time payments in the correct amount, you will be eligible to apply for new federal loans. To bring your loan out of a default status, you will need to make 12 consecutive timely payments. Once your loan is out of default, you can then apply for a deferment. Throughout the repayment period and until a loan or deferment of some type is granted, you will need to continue to make payments.

After your student loan is no longer in default, you should obtain a copy of your credit report. If there is still an entry indicating that your loan is in default, you may want to file a dispute with the credit bureau. After you make 12 consecutive payments, you are entitled to have the default status removed from your credit report. (This is very unique though, and is the only example we know of where the government supports and engages in "credit repair.") Attach a copy of any documentation you have proving that your loan is no longer in default. The credit bureau must investigate within 30 days and must remove derogatory information from your credit report about your student loan that is inaccurate.

Defaulting on your student loans is serious business. Lenders and the Department of Education spend significant resources trying to locate people who have loans that have gone into default. If you are given an opportunity to repay your debt and remove the default status, you should make sure you make each and every payment exactly according to the terms the lender has given you. Otherwise, you will have squandered your chance to get rid of the default.

CHAPTER 4

What to Do When the Debt Collector Calls

What Laws Will Protect You

When you are in debt, sometimes you may feel that you are a sitting duck, waiting for the debt collector to call. What you may not realize, however, is that there are laws which protect debtors from collector practices that you may find troublesome or harassing.

The federal Fair Debt Collections Practices Act (hereafter referred to as the "FDCPA") and other consumer protection laws are written to help consumers. The laws assume that you did not get into debt because you are a deadbeat , but that you fully planned to pay until unforeseen circumstances, such as a job layoff or illness, made it difficult for you to pay your bills. The FDCPA limits how far the debt collector may go to try to collect a debt from you. In fact, under the Act, a debt collector may not act in ways that harass or abuse any person while trying to collect a debt.

Who Has to Follow the FDCPA?

The FDCPA applies only to a collection agency (an agency the original creditor turns your account over to), a creditor collecting for another person, a repossession company, one who buys debts after the debtor fails to pay, or an attorney hired for the purpose of debt collection. Your original creditor—the company that you owe— does not have to follow the FDCPA. But this does not mean original creditors may treat you however they wish. If you feel your original creditor is harassing you, you may be able to sue the creditor for harassment. In addition, the laws of your state may give you protection from both abusive collector and creditor practices.

So what rules does the debt collector have to follow when trying to collect the debt?

Communications Between the Debtor and the Collector

When a collector contacts you to collect a debt, he has to follow certain rules.

Disclosures

The collector has to let you know:

- The amount of the debt.
- The name of the original creditor.
- You have 30 days to dispute that you owe the debt.
- The collector will send you verification that you owe the debt if you dispute it.

A demand for payment will usually be included and sometimes a threat that if payment is not received immediately, the debt will be reported as delinquent, or that the collector may take legal action against you.

Identification

Once the debt collector reaches you by telephone, he must tell you that the call is for the purpose of collecting a debt, and that information provided by you will be used for debt collection purposes. The law also requires that the collector identify that he is calling from a collection agency.

No False Information or Threats

An agency trying to collect a debt from you may not tell you false information to get you to pay. For instance, the collector may not send a letter threatening to sue when he does not intend to sue you, or threatening to sue you before he actually intends to sue. A collector also cannot threaten a debtor in writing, such as sending a letter written in bold print, stating "48-Hour Notice—Warning—Pay This Amount" which a consumer could think of as a threat. Courts have held that a collector demanding payment in five days and describing steps to a lawsuit that the collector threatened to recommend to a creditor misleads the consumer into thinking that a lawsuit will be filed in five days. Similarly, a letter from a creditor identified as a "72-hour notice" threatening legal action within 72 hours is deceptive if he has no intention to sue you in 72 hours. Accordingly, if you receive a letter marked "final notice" from the collector, the collector may not write to you again asking for payment.

In addition, the collector may not impersonate an attorney on the telephone, or send a letter that looks like it is from an attorney or the court when it's not. The collector also may not use a false business name or claim to be calling from the credit bureau, unless the agency he works for is also a credit bureau. You should be wary of a collector who tries to claim that he is a representative of the government or police. Statements such as these are probably not true.

Statements by the collector that he will take your property or garnish your wages sooner than is permitted by law is also considered a deceptive practice. (In most states, property cannot be attached or wages may not be garnished until a collector has sued you and the court rendered judgment in his favor.) Similarly, threats of arrest or imprisonment are prohibited if the collector does not intend to follow through or if the action is illegal. (While debtors may not be put in jail or arrested for owing the majority of debts, arrests and imprisonment could result from failure to pay child support in most states.)

Under the FDCPA, a collector may not demand payment by threatening the consumer, such as a threat to harm the consumer's credit and business reputation.

No Insults

Under the FDCPA, a collector cannot make such statements as, "if you can't pay the hospital bill, you should not have had children," or "if you think what we have been writing is unpleasant, don't challenge us to see what happens if you keep avoiding us!" Use of insulting, discriminatory or belittling language such as "liar," "deadbeat," or "crook" is also not permitted under the Act, including statements that the consumer is financially irresponsible. In addition, the collector may not use obscene or profane language.

Limitations on Where and When to Call

The FDCPA limits where and when a collector can contact you. The debt collector may not communicate with you, including personal visits or telephone calls, at an unusual or inconvenient time. Collection calls to a debtor between 9:00 p.m. and 8:00 a.m. or on Sundays are considered to be unusual and inconvenient. Likewise, the debt collector can't contact you at an unusual place, such as a neighbor's home or hospital.

Collection calls to your place of employment are prohibited if the collector has reason to know that your employer does not allow personal telephone calls. You have the right to tell him not to contact you during the time you are at work because that is an inconvenient time for you to be called.

Finally, a collector cannot call you repeatedly or allow the telephone to ring over and over.

Communications Between the Debt Collector and Third Parties

The debt collector should not call your friends, co-workers, employer or relatives to let them know you owe a debt, without your permission. You have the right to keep this information confidential. This means that the collector may not tell the person who answers the telephone the collection agency's name, unless specifically asked, or state that you owe a debt. However, a collector can contact a third party for help in locating you. In addition, the collector may contact your attorney, your spouse and any co-debtor to discuss your debt.

If the collector sends you mail, the envelope may not show any words, including logo or letterhead, that would let a third party know that the letter is from a collector regarding a debt that you owe. For the same purpose, a collector may not send you a postcard.

How to Get the Debt Collector to Stop Calling You

The FDCPA gives you the power to stop the debt collector from contacting you. To stop the debt collector from calling, you must notify the collector in writing to cease communications with you. Once you send a letter, the collector has to stop contacting you, except to advise you that (1) he is no longer going to try to collect on the debt, or (2) either the collector or creditor plans to take further action against you permissible by law, such as suing you. The debt collector cannot contact you after you tell him not to in writing, to ask for payment.

It is probably a good idea to send a written request by certified mail, return receipt requested. By doing so, you know that the debt collector received your request and the collector could never argue that he was not aware you wanted the communication to stop. The sample letter to the right should be all you need to stop the collection calls and letters.

While you may find it is a relief to have the collection calls stop, you should be

---

Dear Mr. Mist,

For the past three months, I have received several phone calls and letters from you concerning my overdue Rich's Department Store account. As I have informed you, I cannot pay this bill.

Accordingly, under 15 U.S.C., section 1692c, this is my formal notice to you to cease all further communications with me except for the reasons specifically set forth in the federal law.

Very Truly Yours,
Ms. Debtor

Sample Letter from *Money Troubles* by Robin Leonard, Nolo Press 1997 at 8/16 aware that it might not be in your best interest in the long run. For example, by stopping the lines of communication, some collectors feel they are left with no other choice than to proceed with a lawsuit since they can't negotiate with you anymore.

Additionally, you may not have immediate notice of actions that the collector may have taken. For instance, if the collector decides to sue you, the first time you may know about it is when you receive a document from the court. The collector may also decide to sell the debt, unbeknownst to you, and you may have difficulty in trying to work out payment arrangements with the buyer of the debt.

Eventually, you should get notice that the debt has been sold, but there may be a period of time where you don't know who holds your debt, and therefore, with whom you should negotiate payment arrangements. You may find it more helpful to limit the amount of contact the collector has with you, for example, by telling him not to call you at work, rather than stopping all contact with the collector.

What to Do if the Debt Collector Violates the Law

If you feel the debt collector has engaged in practices that you believe are illegal, you can register a complaint with the Federal Trade Commission or complain to your state Consumer Protection Agency.

You may try to get the collector to repeat what he said on the telephone, with witnesses listening. In your letter of complaint, state the date and times of the collector's unlawful behavior. Attach the names of the witnesses who heard the unlawful behavior and the dates and times they heard it. You will probably want to send a copy of the complaint to the original creditor and the collector. It is possible that the creditor will be concerned enough about the illegal practice to erase the debt.

You also have the right to sue a collector for harassment. You would have the greatest chance at winning such a lawsuit if you have documentation of the illegal practice. Without proper evidence or documentation, it is doubtful that a judge would find that the collector engaged in an illegal practice.

Rather than trying to catch the collector on a technical violation of the law, it is always best to focus on negotiating a satisfactory repayment schedule if the debt is valid. Credit counseling agencies like Debt Counselors of America (www.GetOutOfDebt.org) can assist you in doing so if you need help.

Finally, it is important to remember that you are no less of a person because you owe a debt. No one has the right to make you feel as if you are not a worthwhile person. The FDCPA was enacted to protect your dignity.

CHAPTER 5

Forgotten Regulations You Can Use to Make Your Creditors Treat You Fairly

Consumers will be pleased to discover a little known regulation enacted for their protection. This regulation, known as Regulation Z or the Truth in Lending Law, regulates certain credit card practices and helps consumers to know the cost of credit and achieve a fair and timely solution to credit card billing disputes. Each of the questions below is designed to help you understand how Regulation Z works.

When Does Regulation Z Apply?

Regulation Z applies to:

- Credit offered or extended to a consumer;
- Credit used primarily for personal, family or household purposes;
- Credit subject to a finance charge or made payable by a written agreement in more than four installments;
- The advertising of such credit transactions, i.e. credit card applications sent by mail or offered by telephone.

If the offer is for a credit card, then Regulation Z may apply even if there is no finance charge or the credit is not payable by a written agreement in more than four installments.

When Does the Creditor Have to Post My Payment?

The simple answer is as soon as the creditor receives it! How many times have you argued with a creditor over the posting of a payment that you sent on time? If that creditor acted properly, under Regulation Z, any payment you sent must be credited to your account as of the day the creditor actually received the payment, and NOT when the creditor gets around to posting it. If there is a delay in posting the payment, you cannot be charged additional fees. The only exception is when the delay in crediting the payment does not cause you to pay a finance charge.

Suppose, on your monthly statement, the creditor listed certain requirements for you to follow when making a payment, but accepts a payment that does not conform to those requirements? In that case, the creditor still has to credit your payments within five days of receipt, even though you did not follow instructions. For example, assume a creditor has informed the debtor that the payment must be sent along with the account number or payment stub, and the debtor sends a payment but fails to include either the account number or stub. If the creditor accepts the payment anyway, the payment must be credited within five business days of receipt, even though the debtor has failed to follow instructions.

If you always wait until the last minute to send your payments and do not send it so it conforms to your creditors' requirements, your payment might be recorded after the due date and result in a late charge even though it arrived on time.

How Will I Know What the Terms of the Credit Are and if the Amount the Creditor Charges Me Is Correct?

Under Regulation Z, consumers must be told important information about how much the credit will cost them and the terms. When you are given an application or offer to open a credit or charge card account, the card issuer must disclose certain information before you agree to accept the credit offer, including:

- **Annual percentage rate** (how much the credit will cost you, expressed as a yearly rate) and the **Periodic Rate** (how the creditor will determine the finance charge for each billing period).

- **Annual fees** the consumer must pay for issuance of the card or for the availability of credit (usually $25-$50 for regular cards and $75 or more for a "gold" or "platinum" card).

- **User fees (or transaction fees)** the consumer must pay for charging more than the established credit limit, making late payments, using a card to receive a cash advance or set fees a consumer may have to make each month just for having the card.

- **Grace period.** Whether a grace period is provided, allowing the consumer to avoid paying a finance charge by paying the full amount due each month before the due date. If no grace period is provided, consumers must be told up-front.

Knowing this information before deciding whether to accept an offer of credit will help you compare credit offers to decide which offer best suits your needs.

Likewise, creditors have many requirements under Regulation Z for closed-end credit, such as a loan. Before the credit is granted, the creditor must inform the consumer of important terms, some of which include:

- **Total finance charge** - how much the credit will cost you during the time you are using the credit.
- **Amount financed** - a total amount of credit that is being provided to you, including the loan amount, other sums that the creditor has agreed to finance (minus finance charges that the consumer has prepaid).
- **Annual percentage rate** - how much the credit will cost you, expressed as a yearly rate.
- **Variable rate** - information about the terms of the variation, including how much the rate can go up and under what circumstances.
- **Schedule for repayment and total number of payments** - amount and timing of payments.
- **Fees for late payments** - how much the creditor will charge the consumer if payments are made late.
- **Provision demanding full payment** - the circumstances under which the consumer could be required to pay the amount owed in full.

What if I Accidently Pay More Than I Was Supposed to?

If you pay too much, as long as the amount is more than a dollar, the creditor must credit the excess to your account. Or if you prefer, you can send a letter requesting that a refund be sent to you and the creditor must comply within seven days from receiving your written letter. Sometimes this occurs when a consumer sends more than the regular payment; rebates are owed to the consumer or money is owed to the consumer as a result of money that was held on behalf of a consumer. If the creditor does not credit the extra amount to the consumer's account and a finance charge is imposed, the creditor must refund the amount of the finance charge to the consumer's account the next month.

How Often Should I Receive a Statement and What Information Should Be on It?

A consumer should get a statement periodically in the mail, such as monthly or quarterly. The statement should furnish information to the consumer about his account, including:

- How much the consumer owes at the beginning of the billing cycle;
- A list of all transactions occurring on the account during that billing cycle;
- Any amount that may have been credited to the account as a result of payments;
- The amount of finance charges added to total;
- The outstanding balance at the end of the billing cycle;
- The date the consumer must make a payment to avoid further finance charges;
- An address where the consumer can contact the creditor to ask questions about the bill.

What if I Think the Creditor Made a Mistake on My Bill?

The billing error procedure (also called the Fair Credit Billing Act) applies to all open-ended credit accounts and consumer credit cards. A consumer who thinks that an error has occurred on a bill should put the concerns in written form to the creditor at the address given on the statement within 60 days after receiving the incorrect bill. The letter should include:

- The consumer's name;
- The account number; and
- An explanation of why the consumer thinks the bill is wrong, including the type, date and amount of the error.

The consumer should receive an acknowledgment that the creditor has received the consumer's letter and the matter should be addressed within two billing cycles.

Until the billing error is resolved, the consumer may not have to pay any part of a payment that is due, including finance charges, if the consumer thinks the amount that is due is related to the amount that is being disputed. During this time, creditors should not try to collect the payment and may not report, or threaten to report, the failure to pay so that a person's credit is adversely affected.

If, after an investigation, the creditor concludes that the bill is correct, he must provide an explanation to the consumer as to why the creditor believes that the bill is accurate. If the consumer asks, the creditor should give the consumer documentation showing the paperwork that the creditor relied on in making the decision. The consumer must be told when payment is due and how much the consumer still owes in writing (no additional finance charges may be added during this time). The creditor cannot report the consumer as delinquent for the entire time period the creditor has given the consumer to make payment or for ten days, whichever is longer. After that time, the creditor has the right to report to the credit bureau that the consumer has not made payment on time. A creditor can also report adverse information if the consumer does not pay and still claims that the bill is wrong, and if the creditor:

- Reports to the credit bureau that the amount owed is still being disputed;
- Tells the consumer in writing the name and address of everyone the creditor notified that the payment has not been made; and
- Immediately contacts everyone he had previously notified of the delinquency once a resolution occurs.

Once the creditor has engaged is the dispute process described, he does not have to investigate further if the consumer still claims that there is a billing error. The consumer who still believes, for a good reason, that an error has occurred may want to contact the state consumer protection office for further help.

If, instead, the creditor determines that an error has been made, the creditor must correct the error within two billing cycles. The consumer's account should be credited and the consumer should be notified of the result.

Does Regulation Z Give any Special Protection to Homeowners Who Have Used Their Home as Collateral?

Absolutely. Home equity loans or home improvement loans are common examples of a type of loan where the consumer may use his home for collateral. In this situation, a creditor lends money to a consumer who has placed his house as collateral. If the consumer does not pay the debt, the lender can then sell the consumer's house for payment. The intent of Regulation Z was to assist homeowners who may be in danger of losing their home if they default without realizing the ramifications of their actions. Under the "rescission rights" portion of the law, homeowners generally have three days after entering into a contract where they have put their house up for collateral to change their mind or "rescind" the contract without needing a reason. The provision is intended to give the consumer the chance to reconsider his decision before he risks losing his home. In any transaction where rescission is a possibility, the creditor should give notice to the consumer on a separate piece of paper which explains how the consumer can rescind the agreement.

Under certain circumstances, a homeowner may have up to three years to rescind the contract where:

- The consumer has not sold the home, and

- Important disclosures were not made to the consumer at the time the original transaction took place.

A consumer who wants to rescind an agreement should notify the creditor in writing. Notice is considered to be given when the consumer mails the letter.

Regulation Z was passed to help consumers understand the terms and conditions surrounding the extension of credit. You may find it helpful to have your own copy of Regulation Z to refer to as questions arise. If you would like to obtain your own copy of Regulation Z, call the Federal Reserve Board at 202-452-3867 and request that they send a copy.

CHAPTER 6

Beware of the IRS if You Settle or Default on a Debt

IRS regulations could cost you money if you settle a debt with certain creditors or you default on a debt and the creditor writes it off. The rule applies to banks, credit unions, savings and loan associations, and all other financial institutions that have the authority to receive deposits and make loans on amounts of $600 or more.

Debts You Settle

If a financial institution agrees to forego at least $600 of a debt you owe, the IRS will consider the amount you didn't pay as income to you. The creditor will be required to send you and the IRS a Form 1099-C or 1099-A at the end of the tax year. These forms are for the report of miscellaneous income, which means that when you file your tax return for the year in which your debt was forgiven, you must include on your return the "income" amount on the Form 1099-C or 1099-A. Most debtors receive a Form 1099-C or a 1099-A after negotiating the following kinds of settlements: a mortgage lender forgiving the balance owed after a short-sale of a home or a foreclosure sale, a car lender forgiving the balance due after a repossession sale, or a credit card issuer taking less than the full amount owed on an outstanding bill.

Debts Written Off

Increasingly, creditors issue a Form 1099-C or 1099-A after writing off a bad debt, that is, ending collection efforts (including selling the debt to a collection agency) and getting a tax break for the income lost. The IRS requires that financial institutions holding bad debts write them off at the latest three years after default, however, a financial institution may establish an earlier date as long as it applies that earlier date to all debtors. A bank, for example, cannot write off some debts a year after default and other debts three years after.

Creditors and collection agencies increasingly use the threat of 1099 income to try to get debtors to pay up. Often, just before writing off a debt, a creditor will send a letter stating something like, "This is a final demand for payment. If you do not pay the full balance within 30 days, your account will be written off and the IRS will be notified. You may experience a tax liability because of your delinquency." The following January, you are likely to receive a Form 1099-C or 1099-A, and you will have to report the amount written off as income. To add insult to injury, the IRS and credit industry have taken the position that a business that holds your bad debt (such as a collection agency that buys it from a creditor) can still try to collect from you, even though the debt has been written off. If, after listing the income on your tax return, you make any payments on the debt or the creditor sues you and seizes some of your property to satisfy the debt, you will have to file an amended tax return to get any refund due to you.

Exceptions

There are five exceptions stated in the Internal Revenue Code, three of which apply to consumers. Even if the financial institution issues a Form 1099-C or 1099-A, you do not have to report the income if:

- The cancellation or writing off of the debt is intended as a gift (this would be unusual); or
- You discharge the debt in bankruptcy; or
- You were insolvent at the time the creditor waived or wrote off the debt.

For example, let's say your credit card balance reaches $5,000 and you can't afford to pay it. After several conversations with your bank's collections department, you agree to pay $2,600 to settle the entire bill. The January after the bank gets your check, it sends you (and the IRS) a Form 1099-C showing that you "earned" $2,400—the amount your bank forgave you to settle the debt. When you file your tax return that April, you must include the $2,400 as part of your total income unless you discharge the debt in bankruptcy or can show that you were insolvent.

The Internal Revenue Code does not define what is meant by insolvent. Generally, it means that your debts exceed the value of your assets at the time the debt was settled or written off. Therefore, to figure out whether or not you are insolvent, you will have to total up your assets and your debts, including the debt that was forgiven.

Let's say your assets are worth $35,000 and your debts total $45,000. You are insolvent to the tune of $10,000. If any debts are forgiven or written off up to that amount, you will not have to count the Form 1099-C or 1099-A income as part of your income for the year. You will have to initially include the amount on your tax return, but then you can back it out. (A tax preparer can help you do this.) You will have to attach supporting documentation, such as a statement of your assets and liabilities at the time of the settlement or write off. If you simply list the income and then back it out without documentation, expect an IRS audit or adjusted bill.

Continuing, let's say your assets are still worth $35,000 and your debts still total $45,000, but your creditor forgives a $14,000 debt. This time, you will have to initially include the entire $14,000 on your tax return, but then you can back out $10,000, meaning that $4,000 will be included as part of your income. Again, you will need to attach a statement of assets and liabilities.

While most people qualify as insolvent, many people do not. You may be particularly vulnerable if you have an IRA, 401(k), 403(b), Keogh plan or other retirement plan you don't want to use to pay the debt because you need the money for retirement and would be hit with a substantial penalty for early withdrawal. In fact, one common scenario is the person whose house has depreciated in value, who walks away from it owing the bank a chunk of money (let's say $50,000) and whose only other asset is a sizeable retirement fund, such as $65,000 in a 401(k). The last thing the person wants to do is take the 401(k) money and fork it over to the bank. But strictly speaking, that person is not insolvent (assuming no other debts or assets) and would have to report the $50,000 as income for the year, boosting his tax liability by $15,500 (assuming a 31% tax bracket).

If your debts are enormous and your financial institution is willing to settle for less than you owe, it could cost you a lot in the end. Similarly, if you owe a lot and plan on walking away from your debts, your liability may shift to the IRS. Before taking a settlement or turning your back to your creditors, have a tax preparer calculate your tax liability including any likely Form 1099-C or 1099-A income. If your tax bill will be too high and you cannot prove you are insolvent, you may file for bankruptcy and discharge the entire debt. If you decide to go that route, timing becomes an important issue. Be sure to file for bankruptcy before April 15 of next year. Before that date, your debt more than likely qualifies as a dischargeable debt in bankruptcy. After that date, it becomes a part of your income tax liability and won't be dischargeable in bankruptcy for quite some time, if ever.

And bear in mind this fact: even if you don't get a Form 1099-C or 1099-A from a creditor, the creditor may very well have submitted one to the IRS. You can take the risk that the creditor did not pass the information on to the IRS and "forget" to list the income when you file your tax return. But if the IRS has the information, it will send you a tax bill, or worse, an audit notice.

CHAPTER 7

Nine Ways to Improve Your Credit Profile

For most of us, it's a mystery: you fill out a credit card application, send it in, cross your fingers, and hope for the best. And, with most lenders, chances are about 50/50 that you'll get a card. That's because many issuers turn down about half of the applications they get. And just because you get a pre-approved offer doesn't mean you'll get the card. Even pre-approved applications will be evaluated before a card is mailed.

What can you do to maximize the chances that your application for credit will make it into the "yes" pile?

Most credit card companies, as well as many other lenders, use credit scoring systems to help them decide who gets credit and who doesn't. A credit scoring system works like this: a lender takes a look at its customer base and compares those borrowers who have paid their bills on time with those who haven't. Using sophisticated computer programs, they try to figure out what factors those customers have in common. For example, the lender may discover that people who move frequently are less likely to pay their bills on time than people who stay put. If that's the case, then they will look at how long new applicants have been at their current address in their scoring systems.

Credit scoring has become so sophisticated that many times when you apply for a credit card, your application is reviewed and evaluated by a computer, rather than a person. It may sound spooky, but in fact, lenders can review and approve a lot more applications that way. It doesn't mean these programs are perfect, though. If you have unusual circumstances like a recent illness with high medical bills, a divorce that hurt you financially, or other problems, you may find it very frustrating to try to get credit because you don't "look" like everyone else, credit-wise. Even then, however, there are almost always things you can do to improve your credit and your score.

Scoring programs will usually evaluate information in your credit report and your application. It's the information in your credit report that carries the most weight, though, so you'll really want to make sure that it's complete and accurate. Chapter 8 covers fixing credit report errors in depth.

Here are some of the factors that are most likely to be considered for a credit score, and strategies for using them to your advantage:

1. **Checking and Savings Accounts:** Having both a checking and a savings account can improve your credit score. Don't worry about how much money you have in these accounts, it's really just important that you have one of each.

2. **Major Credit Cards:** It's essential that you have at least one major credit card, like a Visa, MasterCard, Discover, or American Express card. Two are even better. Having a major credit card, paid on time of course, is one of the best ways to boost your score. If you don't have a major credit card, consider getting a secured one. You'll be amazed how much it helps.

3. **Credit References:** When it comes to credit scoring, having credit is definitely better than not having it. Even if you're really careful with your money, and have avoided debt all your life, if you don't have credit cards, your score will suffer. Generally, having three or four credit accounts, including one or two major credit cards, is good. Mortgages, car loans and department store cards, as long as they are reported to the major credit bureaus, can help. (Many gasoline cards and small, local department store cards are not reported unless you don't pay.) Finance company loans, though, can actually hurt your score, so steer clear.

4. **Payment Record:** Paying your bills on time is one of the best things you can do to help your score. It really doesn't matter whether you pay off your accounts in full each month, or can only afford the minimum due. What's most important is that you mail those checks on time! If you've had late payments in the past, try from here on to make sure they're paid promptly. Eventually, the older, negative information will become less important.

5. **Employment:** With most lenders, you'll score better if you've been in the same job or working at the same company for at least a couple of years. That doesn't mean you should stick with a job you don't like just to improve your credit score. But it does mean that if you are planning to leave your current employer and think you'll need to apply for credit in the next year or so, do it now.

6 Address: Similar to your job, lenders generally want to see that you've been living at the same address for a couple of years. This isn't always the case, though. In particular, lenders really like to target people who have just moved for new credit cards. Like employment, though, it's stability that lenders want to see, and living at the same place can help demonstrate it. Also, homeowners may score better than renters.

7 Inquiries: Every time you apply for credit and someone looks at your credit report, an "inquiry" is added to your file. It doesn't matter whether or not your application was approved, what matters is the fact that someone accessed your credit report recently. Usually, more than four or five inquiries in the previous six months will count against you. So, if you're looking for a loan, be careful how many applications you submit. Once inquiries are on your credit report, you can't remove them, but after six months they probably won't count against you.

8 Debt: It's amazing how much credit card debt some people can rack up—and then still get lots of offers for more. But, if you want to refinance your debts and obtain lower interest rates, having too much debt may be a problem. There are two things that lenders may consider here: how much debt you have in comparison to your income as reported on your application (your "debt-to-income ratio") and how close you are to your available credit limits. Since every lender is different, it's hard to say how much is too much, but paying down your debts can only help improve your financial life.

9 Collection Accounts, Judgments, or Liens: These can be real red flags to lenders. Many will turn down your application if you have one of these accounts with an unpaid, outstanding balance. Make every effort to get them paid off as quickly as possible. Once you do, check your credit report to make sure they are listed as "paid" on your report.

By the way, every scoring system is different, because they are designed based on a particular lender's experience with borrowers. And, no, you can't get a copy of your credit score—they're kept tightly under wraps. Just keep your credit report in the best shape possible, and if you are turned down, apply somewhere else. Of course, remember not to apply more than four or five times within a six-month period!

"It took a lot of work, but this credit report is truly a masterpiece."

CHAPTER 8

Ten Ways to Repair Your Credit

Having bad credit—marks on your credit report of anything from a late payment or default to a repossession, foreclosure, lien, judgment or bankruptcy—often feels like the end of the world. Let your imagination wander for a moment or two, and you can probably conjure up the worst—employers won't hire you, landlords won't rent to you, banks won't loan you money for a house or car, and credit card issuers certainly won't shower you with offers of plastic. Rarely does anyone with bad credit suffer all these ills. But still, it's no picnic either, and while you probably can get credit, you may pay through the nose for it.

You can end that cycle by rebuilding—repairing, reestablishing, fixing, redeeming, whatever you want to call it—your credit. Creditors certainly review an entire credit history when deciding whether or not to extend credit, but they emphasize recent information. A line showing 12 months of incurring credit and paying on time will weigh more heavily than a five-year-old bankruptcy.

The following is a list of ten easy steps you can take to repair your credit.

1. Create a Spending Plan

Take a month or two to make lists of every outlay of cash or cash equivalent used to make purchases or pay bills, such as check or debit card. Also, track your income for those months. At the end, list every category of expense, and then write down the total amount per month (taking an average if you tracked expenses for two months) you spent in that category. Debt Counselors of America® has an online program called On-Track^{SM} to help you track expenses and compare yourself to others in the same income bracket.

You are now ready to make a spending plan. One goal is to generate enough cash each month to put toward savings—a necessary step in rebuilding your credit. Your list indicates how much you project spending each month.

If the total exceeds your income or leaves you with little left over, you'll have to cut back. For example, if you love to read and spend a lot on books, you can reduce that amount by checking books out from the library or buying only at used bookstores. If you go out to lunch everyday, consider bringing your lunch.

2. Review Your Credit Report

You can order your consolidated credit report through the DCA website at www.GetOutOfDebt.org. The second major step in repairing your credit is cleaning up your credit report. As you read through it, make a list of everything that is incorrect, out-of-date or misleading. In particular, look for:

- Incorrect or incomplete name, address or phone number
- Incorrect Social Security number or birthdate
- Incorrect, missing or outdated employment information
- Incorrect marital status (a former spouse listed as your current spouse)
- Bankruptcies older than ten years or not identified by the specific chapter of the bankruptcy code
- Lawsuits or judgments older than seven years
- Paid tax liens or criminal records older than seven years, delinquent accounts older than seven years or that omit the date of the delinquency
- Credit inquiries older than two years
- Unauthorized credit (not promotional) inquiries (Credit bureaus usually do not remove these at a consumer's request, but it never hurts to ask.)
- Commingled accounts (credit histories for someone with the same name)
- Duplicate accounts (a debt is listed twice, once under the creditor and once under a collection agency)
- Premarital debts of your current spouse attributed to you
- Lawsuits you were not involved in
- Incorrect account histories, such as a late payment notation when you paid on time or a debt shown as past due when it was discharged in bankruptcy

- Paid tax, judgment, mechanic's or other liens listed as unpaid
- A missing notation when you disputed a charge on a credit card bill
- Closed accounts incorrectly listed as open, and
- Accounts you closed that don't indicate "closed by consumer"

Once you've compiled your list, complete the request for reinvestigation form that came with your credit report or type a letter describing every problem. Send your letter to the address provided by the credit bureau for disputing information. Enclose copies of any documents you have that support your claim. Once the credit bureau receives your letter, it must:

- Complete its investigation within 30 days of receiving your letter
- Contact the creditor reporting the information you dispute within five days
- Review and consider all relevant information submitted by you
- Remove all inaccurate and unverified information
- Adopt procedures to keep the information from reappearing
- Reinsert the information only if the creditor certifies that it is accurate and notifies you within five days of the reinsertion, and
- Provide you with the results of its reinvestigation, including a new credit report, within five days of completion.

If the credit bureau claims that the creditor reporting the information verified its accuracy, contact the creditor. Explain that it is incorrect and demand that it be removed. Creditors who report information to credit bureaus must:

- Not report information they know is incorrect
- Not ignore information they know contradicts what they have on file
- Notify credit bureaus when you dispute information
- Note when accounts are "closed by the consumer"
- Provide credit bureaus with the month and year of the delinquency of all accounts placed for collection, charged off or similarly treated, and
- Finish their investigation of your dispute within 30 days.

If the creditor will not remove the incorrect information, call the credit bureau reporting it directly for help:

Equifax 800-685-1111

Experian 888-397-3742

Trans Union 800-851-2674

If you get nowhere, you have the right to put a 100-word statement in your file explaining your dispute. Don't always assume that adding a 100-word statement is the best approach. In fact, it's often wiser to simply explain the negative mark to future creditors than to try to explain it in 100 words or less. If you do add a 100-word statement, be sure to link it to a specific entry in your credit report so the statement comes out when the disputed information comes out.

3. Add Positive Account Histories to Your Credit Files

Often, credit reports don't include accounts that you might expect to find. Some major commercial lenders don't report mortgages or car loans. Local banks or credit unions often don't provide information to credit bureaus. If your credit file is missing information for accounts you pay on time, send the credit bureaus a copy of a recent account statement and copies of canceled checks showing your payment history. Ask the credit bureaus to add the information to your file. While they aren't required to do so, they might, and they may also charge you a fee.

4. Add Information Showing Stability to Your Credit File

Creditors like to see evidence of stability in your file. If any of the items listed below are missing, send a letter to the credit bureaus asking that the information be added. Enclose any documentation that verifies information you're providing, such as your driver's license, a canceled check, a bill addressed to you, a pay stub showing your employer's name and address or anything else similar.

- Current employment (employer's name and address and your job title)
- Previous employment if you've had your current job for less than two years
- Current residence, and if you own it
- Previous residence if you've been at your current place for less than two years

- Telephone number, especially if it's unlisted
- Date of birth
- Social Security number, or
- Bank checking or savings account number.

Again, credit bureaus aren't required to add this information, but they often do.

5. Get Credit in Your Own Name

If you are married, separated or divorced, you're entitled to a credit report issued in your own name. This is an excellent strategy for repairing your credit if:

- All or most of your financial problems can be attributed to your spouse or former spouse; or
- You and your spouse have gone through financial difficulties together, but most credit was in your spouse's name only.

Even if both of you have had financial problems, separating your credit histories can help you both repair your credit. Contact all three credit bureaus and ask that a credit file be created in your name only. Then insist that the credit bureaus remove all accounts belonging to your spouse alone. If you want to obtain credit in your own name, complete credit applications in your name only.

6. Combine Your Credit History With Your Spouse's

If you are married, you and your spouse can ask that your credit histories be merged. If you have bad credit and your spouse has good credit, getting his or her credit histories into your file may be just what you need.

Write to the three credit bureaus and request that they merge your files. Once your request is complete, your file will contain your negative marks and your spouse's positive ones. Your spouse must then write the credit bureaus to have your credit accounts removed from his or her file. (Step 5)

7. Get Credit Cards and Use Them Wisely

Using a credit or department store card will improve your credit history quickly. Most credit reports show payment histories for 24-36 months. If you charge something every month and make your payments on time, your credit report will show steady and proper use of revolving credit.

If you don't currently have a credit card, apply for one. It's often easiest to obtain a card from a department store or gasoline company. These companies usually open your account with a very low credit line. Once you have your first card, apply for a regular credit card from a bank, such as a Visa, MasterCard or Discover card. You may be eligible only for a card with a low credit line or high interest rate. If you make your payments on time, however, after a year or so you can apply for an increase in your line of credit or a reduction of the interest rate.

If you don't qualify for a regular credit card, consider one of the following:

- **Co-signed or guaranteed account.** Someone else promises to repay if you default. Be sure that the payment history is reported for both you and the co-signer or guarantor, not just the co-signer or guarantor.

- **Authorized user account.** Someone will add you to an account as an authorized user; you can use the credit line but you are not responsible for repaying the charges. Again, make sure the payments are reported for you.

- **Secured credit card.** You deposit a sum of money with a bank and are given a credit card with a credit limit for a percentage of the amount you deposit.

8. Open Deposit Accounts

Creditors look for bank accounts as a sign of stability. They also look for bank accounts as a source of how you will pay your bills. If you fill out a credit application and cannot provide a bank account number, you won't be given credit.

A savings account, too, will improve your standing with creditors. Even if you never deposit additional money into the account, creditors assume that people who have savings accounts use them. Having an account reassures creditors of two things: You are making an effort to build up savings, and if you don't pay your bill and the creditor sues you, it has a source to collect.

9. Work With Local Merchants

Another way to repair your credit is to approach a local merchant (such as a furniture store) and arrange to purchase an item on credit. Many local stores will work with you in setting up a payment schedule, but be prepared to put down a deposit of up to 30% or to pay a high rate of interest. If you still don't qualify, the merchant might agree to give you credit if you get someone to co-sign or guarantee the loan, or you may be able to get credit by first buying an item on layaway.

10. Obtain a Bank Loan

Take some money you've saved and open a savings account. Ask the bank for a loan against the money in your account. If the bank doesn't offer these types of loans, apply for a personal loan and offer either a co-signer or to secure it against some collateral you own. In either case, make sure the bank reports the loan payments to credit bureaus.

A Word About Credit Repair Clinics

It's simple. Avoid these outfits. Many of their practices are illegal. Some have been caught stealing the credit files or Social Security numbers of people who are under 18, have died or live in out-of-the-way places like Guam or the U.S. Virgin Islands, and substituting these for the files of people with poor credit histories.

Other credit clinics break into credit bureau computers and change or erase bad credit files. Still others suggest that you create a new identity by applying for an IRS Employer Identification number (EIN), a nine-digit number that resembles a Social Security number, and use it instead of your Social Security number. Not only is this illegal, but by using an EIN, you won't earn Social Security benefits.

These methods are just the tip of the iceberg. Credit repair clinics devise new schemes as often as consumer protection agencies catch onto their previous ones. Even assuming a credit repair company is legitimate, these companies can't do anything for you that you can't do yourself. What they will do, however, is charge you between $250 and $5,000 for their unnecessary services.

Federal law regulates for-profit credit repair clinics. Under the federal law, a credit repair clinic must:

- Inform you of your rights under the Fair Credit Reporting Act
- Accurately represent what it can and cannot do

- Not collect any money until all promised services are performed
- Provide a written contract, and
- Let you cancel the contract within three days of signing.

Even with these regulations, you're better off steering clear.

CHAPTER 9

How to Use the Credit Reporting Law to Help You Get and Keep Good Credit

If you've ever found a mistake on your credit report, you may have found it more than a little frustrating trying to straighten it out. Although credit reports still aren't perfect, the good news is that they're getting better, and you have a lot more leverage than you used to if you discover a problem. That's because in 1996, Congress passed a new law designed to make credit reports more accurate and complete. That law is called the Consumer Credit Reporting Reform Act of 1996 and it amended the Fair Credit Reporting Act.

Here's how the new law can help you fix your credit report and keep it in better shape.

Accuracy
This section effective 9-30-97

The Old Law
Credit reporting agencies (also called "credit bureaus") were supposed to investigate mistakes consumers brought to their attention within "a reasonable time period" which sometimes stretched on for a long time. Also, the rules about how they were to handle those investigations weren't very specific.

The New Law
If you dispute something in your report, the credit bureau generally has 30 days to investigate and correct it, if it's wrong. If you give the bureau any relevant information or proof to back up your side of the story, the bureau has to consider it, and also has to supply that documentation to the company that reported the information in the first place. When the investigation is completed, the bureau has to send

the results to you within five business days, along with a notice about your rights under the credit reporting law. If corrections were made to the credit report, the bureau must send you a corrected copy.

The Old Law

If you found a mistake, it was your responsibility to track down all the reporting agencies that might have the wrong information and correct it with each of them. This could be very time-consuming.

The New Law

Credit reporting agencies are required to use an automated system so that if you dispute information and it's corrected by the lender, that correction will be shared with all the other bureaus that may have the information.

The Old Law

If you told the bureau that there was incorrect information in your report and the bureau fixed it, there was nothing to prevent that same wrong information from being put right back on your credit report. Consumers with common names or those who had been the victims of credit fraud sometimes found themselves fighting about the same inaccurate information over and over again.

The New Law

Reporting agencies are required to use reasonable procedures to keep information that has been deleted from reappearing on credit reports. In fact, if you dispute information and the bureau deletes it, it's not allowed to put it back on your report unless a) the company that supplied the information to the credit bureau certifies it is correct, and b) within five business days, the credit bureau provides you with a notice including the name, address and phone number of the company supplying the information. The bureau is also required to give you a notice describing how you can add an explanatory statement to your file explaining your side of the story.

The Old Law

Lenders and other companies that supplied information about consumers to credit reporting agencies weren't even mentioned in the old law. This put the credit bureau in the middle of disputes, and meant that if a company persisted in reporting inaccurate information about one of your accounts, there wasn't much you could do to force them to stop.

The New Law

Creditors and other companies that furnish information are not allowed to provide information they "know or consciously avoid knowing" is inaccurate. If you or the credit bureau bring a mistake to a furnisher's attention, it is required to quickly investigate and correct it if it's found to be wrong. Plus, the lender must make the correction with all the bureaus that were given the original information, saving you the hassle of trying to contact all of them. Also, if you notify the lender that it has wrong information about your account, it has to report that the information is under dispute when it supplies it to a reporting agency.

Closed Accounts
This section effective 9-30-97

The Old Law
There was nothing that required lenders to tell the bureau when a customer closed an account. So it wasn't unusual for consumers to find that their credit report listed old accounts they had closed as open.

The New Law
If you close an account, the creditor has to tell the reporting agencies that you've closed it, and the reporting agencies then have to list the account as closed at your request on your report. This can help improve your credit report if you have too many lines of credit open and available. Of course, if you just stop using a credit card and don't tell the issuer you want it closed, it won't be reported as closed.

Just cutting up your card and tossing it in the trash also won't close your credit card account. The safest way to close a credit card account is by sending a certified letter, return receipt requested to the customer service department of the card issuer. Ask the card issuer to close your account and to report your account to credit bureaus as "closed by consumer." In approximately ten days, the card issuer should send you a letter confirming that your account is "closed by the consumer." If you don't receive the confirmation letter, follow up by calling the card issuer to make sure it closed your card and is reporting it properly to the credit bureaus. You may even want to get another copy of your credit report to make sure it is reported correctly. To receive a consolidated credit report, be sure to visit www.credit.com.

Disclosures
This section effective 9-30-97

The Old Law
It wasn't uncommon for lenders to refuse to show consumers their own credit reports. You might have been turned down for a loan at a car dealer, for example, and the finance officer would tell you that there were problems on your report, but if you wanted to see it, you had to order your own copy and wait (sometimes several weeks) until it arrived. The reason for this was that bureaus thought consumers might get confused if they saw the lender's version of their credit report, which was even more confusing than the already confusing consumer version!

The New Law
Bureaus can't prohibit lenders from showing consumers their own reports, as long as the consumer has been denied credit or some other benefit as a result of something in the report.

Employment
This section effective 9-30-97

The Old Law
Employers were allowed to review your credit report without your knowledge or permission.

The New Law
Employers must get your written permission before accessing your report. And before you're denied a job, promotion or some other benefit because of information in your credit report, the employer has to give you a copy along with a notice about your rights.

Free Reports
This section effective 9-30-97

The Old Law
You could get a free report within 30 days only if you were denied credit or some other benefit due to information in your report.

The New Law
You are still entitled to a free credit report if you are turned down for credit, but you have 60 days to request it. Also, you can also get a free credit report if you are unemployed and intend to apply for employment within 60 days; you are on public welfare; you believe you're a victim of credit fraud; or you have been notified by a collection agency affiliated with a credit bureau that your credit rating may be negatively affected. Otherwise, a copy of your report will cost about $8 (adjusted each year for inflation).

Inquiries
This section effective 9-30-97

The Old Law
"Inquiries" refers to the list of companies that have seen your credit report in the past two years. Credit bureaus used to be required to tell you who had accessed your report in the past six months for credit reasons, or the past two years for

employment reasons. However, the law didn't say anything about how those listings should read. So, what consumers often got was a list of coded or abbreviated names, sometimes impossible to decipher. It's important to be able to tell who has looked at your credit report in case it has been illegally accessed.

The New Law
Reporting agencies now must list the full name or complete business name of anyone who reviewed your report in the past two years for employment reasons, or in the past year for any other reason. And, if you ask for it, they must tell you the address and telephone number of anyone listed as an inquiry.

Negative Information
This section effective 1-1-98

The Old Law
Generally, negative information like late payments, collection accounts, or charge-offs, can only be reported for seven years. However, the old law wasn't very clear about when that seven-year period started. So some people found this type of negative information reported for a very long time.

The New Law
For information added to a credit report beginning January 1, 1998, the new law is much clearer about how the seven-year time frame works. Bureaus are allowed to report collection, profit-and-loss, charged-off or similar accounts, for seven years beginning 180 days after the payment should have been made. Suppose, for example, you have a payment that was due January 1, 1998, but you've stopped paying, and the account is turned over to a collection agency in June 1998. The credit bureau can report that account, both the one with the original creditor, as well the one with the collection agency, for only seven years plus 180 days beginning January 1, 1998 (the original due date). Now, of course, if you get caught up and then later fall behind, that can start a whole new reporting time frame.

Pre-Approved Credit Offers
This section effective 9-30-97

The Old Law
You've probably at some time received offers for preapproved credit cards. This is the way it works: a lender asks the credit bureau to run a list of names through its databases and sort out the ones that meet the lender's qualifications. Those who pass this "prescreening" are sent a preapproved offer. The old law didn't specifically talk about preapproved offers. So, the Federal Trade Commission interpreted the law and said that lenders who used prescreening were required to send a "firm"

offer of credit to everyone who passed the prescreen. This meant that, unless you had declared bankruptcy, gone to jail or something else extremely unusual had happened in the meantime, you were supposed to get the card if you wanted it.

The New Law

Lenders are still allowed to use prescreening to select customers for offers and they are still required to make a firm offer of credit to anyone who passes. But, they are also allowed to create a secret list of additional qualifications that can be considered before a card is actually given. So, if you say "yes" to a preapproved offer, you may still be turned down based on those other criteria. Essentially, this means that "preapproved" is really just pre-selected, not preapproved.

Tip: If you don't like the idea of your credit file being reviewed for these kinds of offers, you can call one of the major credit bureaus to place a prescreening block on your file. In theory, each bureau must share your request with the others, but to be safe, you should call all three. Contact Equifax at 800-566-4711; Experian at 800-353-0809; or Trans Union at 800-680-7293.

CHAPTER 10

Credit Scoring: How It Works and Actions You Can Take to Improve Your Score

What Is Credit Scoring?

If you have tried to get credit, a loan or a mortgage, you may have had your credit information graded for risk potential. This is called "credit scoring" or "risk scoring." Credit scoring is one factor that lenders or creditors consider to determine if they should give you a loan, a mortgage, or extend you credit. According to research, the better a borrower's score, the more a borrower is able and willing to repay a loan. The "score" is a number grade affixed to a consumer's credit history at a particular point in time. Lenders use credit scoring to speed up the loan review process and to reduce the cost of examining a consumer's credit information. Credit scoring also gives lenders a non-biased method to evaluate the credit history of a borrower.

Credit scoring occurs at many levels. Each credit bureau has a credit scoring model based on that particular bureau's data on the borrower. Although each bureau has a different name for the credit scoring product (Equifax provides Beacon; Trans Union provides EMPIRICA, and Experian/TRW provides TRW/FICO®), all use the Fair Isaac Company's (FICO) model. The scores are scaled consistently across the bureaus so that scores at all three bureaus should be similar. In addition to credit bureau scores, there are numerous other company scoring models, such as "application scores," which lenders calculate directly. "Custom scoring models" are developed from a business's own data on its customers, such as information from credit application forms and credit reports. This article will concentrate on the FICO scoring model.

How Does Credit Scoring Work?

Credit scoring places a value on the types of accounts you hold as well as your history. The formula that determines your score is not disclosed to the consumer. However, a consumer can determine what information is important in scoring models by knowing what information is put into a FICO® score and knowing the four "reason codes" that accompany your score.

Information in a FICO Score

A FICO score is based on the information in your credit report located at that particular credit bureau. It is not based on your assets or income, although lenders consider these factors separately. FICO grades your risk by looking at the entire credit picture:

Your Payment History: FICO considers whether you have accounts in collection; whether you have any delinquencies, and how frequent and recent they are; and whether you make your payments on time. How much impact each item has on your score depends on what other information is in the report. For instance, one late payment may not affect your score significantly if the rest of your history is good, because the model looks at credit patterns, not isolated credit mistakes. In addition, FICO gives you points for maintaining a good payment relationship.

The Amount of Outstanding Debt: FICO considers the number of balances recently reported, the average balance across all trade lines, and the relationship between the total balance and total credit limit. FICO considers your current level of borrowing and whether you are close to or over your limit. Carrying too much credit is held against you even if you do not have balances on those cards.

Your Credit History: FICO looks at how long you have had your account, the total number of "inquiries" and new accounts opened, the number of inquiries and new accounts opened in the last year, and the amount of time since the most recent inquiry. Banks, department stores, employers or landlords make "inquiries" on your credit report every time you apply for credit or a loan at that institution. The FICO scoring model considers inquiries because statistics show that those anticipating financial troubles try to increase the number of credit lines the have available.

The FICO model has taken into account certain lender practices that normally would negatively affect your credit report. For instance, if you were interested in buying a car and the dealer agreed to finance you, the dealer may run credit inquiries on various lenders, which would then show up as numerous inquiries on your credit report. Beginning the first quarter of 1998, FICO models treat all inquiries occurring within a 14-day period as one inquiry. In addition, all models will ignore all auto- and mortgage-related inquires that occur within a 30-day period before calculating your score.

The Types of Credit You Use: FICO® looks at the diversity of credit you use, whether you use bank cards, travel and entertainment cards, department store cards, personal finance company references, and/or installment loans.

Negative Information: Negative information in your credit report that could impact the FICO score includes bankruptcies, delinquencies or late payments on accounts, collections, too many credit lines with maximum available funds borrowed, too little credit history (less than five credit lines in the past two years), and too many credit report inquiries.

Information FICO Does Not Consider: FICO does not consider your race, color, religion, national origin, sex, sexual orientation, marital status, or age.

A typical scoring model may also consider your job or profession for stability, and how long you've lived at your address.

How much weight each of these factors has on your score is not disclosed to consumers because it causes more confusion than insight into the credit scoring process. Everything in credit scoring is relative—one negative item can have a small or large impact on your score depending on your credit history. If you have a long and seasoned history of credit and many established accounts, one late payment would have a small impact on your score. However, if you have a short credit history, one late payment would impact your credit history much more. If you have no established credit, you will have no score. Credit scoring requires that you have at least one account that is older than six months and have at least one account that has been reported to the credit bureau in the last six months (this could be the same account).

Your score should be affected less if you have late payments on minor credit lines versus major ones. For example, if you are delinquent on a gas or department store account, and not on a mortgage or auto loan, your score should not be affected as much as it would if you are delinquent on an auto loan. Your credit score should be stronger with credit cards than mortgages since statistics show that credit cards are more indicative of paying on a loan than a mortgage is (most people will pay on their mortgage no matter what, and let credit card payments slide). Paying on a secured card should affect your score more than payments on department store cards.

The Four Reason Codes

Lenders are not required to tell you your credit score, but if your score is low and you are turned down for a loan, the lender must give you the reasons for your low score. Your score is accompanied by four "reason codes" that explain why your score wasn't higher, listed in order of impact on the score. These codes are essential in helping you improve your score later in time. The following list of all possible FICO reason codes

show how many aspects of your credit report are used in a FICO® score. Your four reason codes would be from the following list:
- Amount owed on accounts is too high
- Delinquency on accounts
- Too few bank revolving accounts
- Too many bank or national revolving accounts
- Too many accounts with balances
- Consumer finance accounts
- Account payment history is too new to rate
- Too many inquiries in last 12 months
- Too many accounts opened in last 12 months
- Proportion of balances to credit limits is too high
- Amount owed on revolving accounts is too high
- Length of revolving credit history is too short
- Time since delinquent is too recent or unknown
- Length of credit history is too short
- Lack of recent bank revolving account information
- No recent non-mortgage balance information
- Number of accounts with delinquency
- Too few accounts currently paid as agreed
- Time since derogatory public record or collection
- Amount past due on accounts
- Serious delinquency, derogatory public record or collection
- Too many bank or national revolving accounts with balances
- No recent revolving balances
- Proportion of loan balances to loan amounts is too high
- Lack of recent installment loan information
- Date of last inquiry too recent
- Time since last account opening is too short
- Number of revolving accounts
- Number of bank revolving or revolving accounts
- Number of established accounts
- No recent bank card balances
- Too few accounts with recent payment information*

*See FICO Scoring "Reasons" Guide at First Rate Mortgage, a division of Planners Financial Services, Inc.

What Is a Good Credit Score?

What actual number is a good score depends on the scoring model, the type of loan, and the lender's acceptable risk level and credit policies. For some models like FICO, the higher the score, the better. For other models, the lower the score, the better. If the score on a borrower's credit report is too low for one product, it may be acceptable for other products. Likewise, if one lender turns down a request for credit, it does not mean that another one will. For instance, an automobile dealer may accept a lower score than a creditor who offers an unsecured line of credit.

FICO® scores range from 375 - 900 points. With mortgage lenders, there is a pattern for acceptable FICO scores. A score of 650 to 675 is considered excellent, and very basic underwriting or information beyond the score will be necessary to get a loan with the most favorable terms. If a borrower gets this score, he or she can get a loan for a mortgage in significantly less time. A score between 620 and 650 is still acceptable, and probably will cause lenders to look more closely at the borrower's file to determine potential risks. Lenders may require supplemental credit documentation and letters of explanation before an underwriting decision is made. If a borrower has a score between these numbers, a mortgage decision will take approximately the same amount of processing time as it took before mortgage companies used FICO scoring. Borrowers with a score below 620 may find themselves locked out of the best loan rates and terms offered by mortgage lenders, or may have to put up a higher down payment, such as 10%.

A credit score can be a significant factor in the loan process, or just one piece of the puzzle, depending on the lender and the type of loan. For instance, a credit score may play a larger role for consumers seeking home equity loans, as the credit score dictates the pricing for the loan. On the other hand, a traditional first mortgage may not put as much emphasis on the credit score.

How Can I Improve My Credit Score?

Your credit score is constantly changing as your credit report information is always changing. Every time you try to get a loan or mortgage, the lender computes a new credit score. Taking steps to improve your credit report may not significantly or immediately impact your credit score since the scoring models study patterns of credit behavior over time. Here are some general tips on how to improve your credit history which, if you follow these steps over time, will improve your FICO score. Keep in mind that as negative information ages, it has less importance. It usually takes one full year of good credit behavior to see a significant change in your credit score. This means you should exhibit a full year of responsible payment behavior in your credit report—specifically, conservative use of credit, paying on time, and not requesting too much credit during a short period of time.

Correct Errors.

You should get a copy of your credit report and make sure all information in it is complete and correct. Keep in mind that any corrections you make to your report takes 30 days to take effect. Again, remember that removing or changing one incorrect derogatory item from your credit report will not guarantee an increase in the score. In addition, many lenders will not count errors on your report if you document those errors for the lender. Consumers can obtain a consolidated credit report from the Debt Counselors of America website, www.getoutofdebt.org

Keep inquiries to a minimum.

Don't "credit surf," or move balances from card to card to take advantage of promotional low interest rates. Many inquiries make it appear that you are shopping for credit, which indicates that you anticipate the need for many lines of credit. The more seasoned and longer your credit history, the better.

Close unneeded accounts.

The less available credit you have, the less risk you will pose to a potential creditor or lender. Keep around two to four credit cards for the best score. Close all unused or unnecessary accounts.

Just cutting up your card and tossing it in the trash does not close your credit card account. The safest way to close a credit card account is by sending a certified letter, return receipt requested, to the customer service department of the card issuer. Ask the card issuer to close your account and to report your account to credit bureaus as "closed by consumer." In approximately ten days, the card issuer should send you a letter confirming that your account is "closed by the consumer." If you don't receive the confirmation letter, follow up by calling the card issuer to make sure it closed your card and is reporting it properly to the credit bureaus. You may even want to get another copy of your credit report to make sure it is reported correctly.

Pay off credit cards.

This shows that you use credit wisely and aren't spreading yourself thin. Keep your credit limits and outstanding balances down. Conservative use of credit is important-keep balances at below 50% of the available credit for credit cards.

Pay credit obligations on time.

The longer history you have of responsibly using credit and paying on time, the better your score.

Satisfy any public records.

Take care of any outstanding items such as tax liens or judgments.

If you receive a bad score, request a copy of the four reason codes and do what you can to address them all.

CHAPTER 11

How to Get All the Cheap Credit You Want

Today, the average person pays around 17% on their credit card balances. While interest charges may seem low when you look at the monthly charge on your statement, over the long run they can really add up. In fact, the average person can put a hundred bucks or more in his or her wallet just by getting a lower rate on a credit card or two. If you're carrying a big balance, you can save even more. Here's how much:

Interest Cost to Pay Off Various Credit Card Balances

	INTEREST RATE		
	19%	15%	11%
$1000	$ 1,706	$ 510	$ 468
$1500	$ 3,610	$1,683	$ 894
$2000	$ 7,415	$3,351	$1,741
$2500	$16,917	$7,514	$3,840

(BALANCE shown on left axis)

Total interest charge, with a 2% minimum payment. *Source:* Zilch software.

So what are you waiting for? Following are some strategies that will help you get all of the cheap credit you want.

Just Ask

A survey done a few years ago found that about half of the people who asked their current credit card issuer for a lower rate, got one. Most credit card issuers have many different programs, some of which may carry lower rates. But if you're paying a higher rate, they probably won't tell you about the lower ones unless you ask.

Call your card issuer and tell them you'd you like to remain a customer but you're going to have to leave if they don't have a program that will give you a better rate. Give the customer service person a break and be friendly. If you don't get an immediate "yes," don't let that discourage you. Ask to talk with a supervisor, or call back another time. (For this strategy to work, you should be paying your bills on time each month.) You might want to sweeten the pot by offering to transfer balances from another card.

Go Fishing

There are some 20,000 credit card programs available today. With that many, you should be able to find at least one that will offer you a good deal. A couple of sources you may want to try: www.cardtrak.com and www.bankrate.com. It can be confusing to sort through so many different programs, but it can be well worth it. If you're confused about whether to choose a low fixed or low variable rate, keep this tidbit in mind: in most cases, a credit card issuer can raise the rate on a fixed card as long as you're given 15 days advance notice. So that means a fixed rate may not necessarily be better if interest rates in the economy go up!

Open the Mail

You're flooded with credit card offers, right? While some may well qualify for the "junk mail" category, occasionally there are a few gems. Look for a low introductory rate that applies to balance transfers until they are paid off, convenience checks that offer a good rate without a high fee, or simply a straightforward low rate. If you're considering a card with a low introductory rate that's only good for a few months, make sure that the "permanent" rate is also attractive or you'll be scrambling to find a new card in a few months.

One more thing to watch out for: due to recent changes in the law, "pre-approved" credit card offers aren't always what they seem. If you respond to one of these offers, the issuer can create a secret list of additional qualifications that can be considered before it actually gives you a card. So, if you say "yes" to a preapproved offer, you may still be turned down based on those other criteria. Essentially, this means that "preapproved" is really just pre-selected, not preapproved.

Improve Your Score

You'll have the best chance of qualifying for the credit you want if you have a good credit score. Credit scores are simply a way that lenders evaluate applications. While every lender of different, there are generally some things you can do to improve your score: close accounts you don't use, make sure you have at least a couple of major credit cards paid on time for the last 18 months or more, submit no more than four or five credit applications in any six-month period, use less than 70 to 80 percent of your available credit limits at any time, and avoid late payments or other negative information.

Consolidate

You may be able to lower your costs by consolidating some or all of your debt. For example, you may be able to transfer more expensive credit card balances to your cards that have cheaper rates. Or, you may find that a home equity loan or a margin loan against your investments offers a better rate than what you're paying. Other options can include loans against retirement plans or life insurance policies. Be very, very careful here. Many people fall into the trap of consolidating their debts and then running up new balances.

This strategy will only work if you are committed to paying off your debts as quickly as possible. So don't blow it. Make sure you have good control of your spending, and a written plan for becoming debt-free in three to five years. Debt Counselors of America offers tools that can help you, including Debt Eliminator® (which offers a detailed plan to get out of debt as quickly as possible), and On-Track℠ (a financial tracking program to help you keep your spending under control). Information about both services is available at www.GetOutOfDebt.org.

If You're Turned Down for a Low-Rate Card...

First, realize you're in good company. Most issuers turn down at least 50% of new applications, and the rejection rate for some with rock-bottom rates can be much higher—even 90%. Now that you're feeling a little better, take a good hard look at that rejection letter. Do you understand the reasons listed for turning you down? Are they clear? Do they apply? If not, call the credit card company and ask for a clear, specific explanation. That way, you'll know what you need to do to improve your credit before you apply again.

If you have been turned down, get a copy of your credit report. It's free if you ask for it promptly. And it's very important to check to make sure it's accurate and up-to-date. Information about how to order it will be listed on the denial letter.

"Hi. I'm looking for a credit card with no limit and an interest rate of 1.2%. Hello? Hello?"

CHAPTER 12

Plastic Power: Strategies for Making the Most of Your Credit Cards

At Debt Counselors of America, we've helped thousands of people with too much debt. So you probably figure we'd think credit cards are terrible, right? Wrong!

Credit cards can be a great tool, and even save you money, if you're smart about how you use them. That doesn't mean charging up a storm on things you can't afford, or even using your cards to maintain your lifestyle. But if you know the benefits of credit cards and how to take advantage of them, you can come out ahead. Here are the advantages of saying "Charge It!"

Other People's Money

When you use your credit card, you're using the lender's money. The question is, how much are you paying for it? If your card has a grace period and you pay the balance in full, then you're paying nothing to use someone else's money for anywhere from a few days to as much as two months, depending on the length of the grace period and when you make your purchase.

Smart Strategy: Time a big purchase a day or two after the closing date of your card's billing cycle to get the maximum float.

What happens if you have to borrow money? A low rate credit card can actually be a great deal. There are plenty of expensive traps on many cards, so be careful. Look for a steady, low-rate card and make sure you pay the bills on time so you don't end up with a late fee or a higher rate.

Smart Strategy: Shop for a low-rate card at **www.cardtrak.com** or **www.consumer-action.com**, or ask your card issuer to lower your current rate.

Protection for Purchases

Use your credit card for purchases and you'll have additional protection you just don't get when you pay by cash or check. You can dispute a charge if merchandise you order is not delivered as agreed (in the wrong quantity, the wrong color, or on the wrong date, for example). You have up to 60 days from the date the card issuer mailed the statement showing the disputed charge to complain.

You can call the card issuer to dispute a charge, but we don't recommend it. You only protect your rights under The Fair Credit Billing Act if you put your complaint in writing to the card issuer at the address listed on the statement for billing errors. We recommend you send your letter by certified mail, return receipt requested. Keep in mind that the law doesn't cover changing your mind—for that you'll have to deal with the merchant directly.

You may also be able to dispute a charge when there is a problem with the *quality* of the goods or services you bought. This is a little trickier, so follow the rules carefully. Here are the basic requirements:

- The charge must be for $50 or more.

- You must have bought the merchandise in your home state or within 100 miles of your billing address.

- You must have made a good faith effort to resolve the problem with the merchant.

In this case, you can't dispute the charge and withhold payment if you've already paid off the charge, so act quickly if you think there is a problem. Again, we recommend you write a letter to the card issuer disputing the charge and send it by certified mail, return receipt requested.

Whether or not you can successfully dispute a charge because of a problem with the quality of the merchandise you bought depends on what rights your state laws give you against the seller of the goods. If, under your state law, you can withhold payment to a seller of defective merchandise, you may be able to withhold payment to your credit card issuer.

Smart Strategy: Use your credit card for big-ticket items, online or mail order purchases, or for any other charge where there could be a potential problem with the merchandise or service. Then, check your credit card statement carefully and dispute any errors in writing immediately.

Protection for Losses

Lose your wallet or purse filled with cash and you may be out of luck. Lose your credit cards, though, and it may be a little hassle getting them replaced, but that's about it.

Under the federal Truth in Lending Act, the most you can be held responsible for is $50 in unauthorized charges. And that's only if your card was actually stolen and used. If someone just steals your card number without taking the card itself, your liability is zero. This is more protection than your debit card provides you.

Smart Strategy: Keep in a safe place a list of your credit card numbers and the phone numbers to call if they are lost or stolen (not in your purse or wallet). Call immediately if you think you've lost them.

Travel Advantages

Whether you're packing for a trip across the state or overseas, don't forget to pack the plastic. Major credit cards are convenient, widely accepted, and offer you additional protections mentioned earlier—both for purchases and in case you and your wallet part ways.

When you venture overseas, you'll find that in many places, American Express, MasterCard and Visa cards will be accepted by many merchants. In some places, they'll prefer plastic over traveler's checks.

Besides the convenience, another advantage to using credit cards overseas is the fact that you'll usually get a better exchange rate than you can on your own through local merchants. Credit card purchases are exchanged at wholesale currency rates, which are usually very attractive. One caveat: Some card issuers tack on a 1% "conversion fee" on foreign credit card purchases, but not all do, so ask in advance.

Smart Strategy: Take your major credit cards with you overseas, but be sure to check your credit card receipts carefully to make sure the amount is correct (foreign currency may sometimes throw you off) and keep a record of your card numbers in case there is a problem.

Car Rental Savings

If you don't have a major credit card or only a debit card, it can be a hassle to rent a car. Some car rental agencies will not allow you to reserve a car with a debit card. (To learn more about the differences between credit and debit cards, see Chapter 13 entitled "Credit Card or Debit Card: The Great Debate.") But if you do have one, you may be able to save a bundle if your card offers free Collision Damage Waiver (CDW) coverage. This allows you to decline the rental agency's expensive coverage. Many premium cards (like gold or platinum) and some standard cards offer this benefit. Just beware: in some countries you may have to buy coverage anyway. Check with the rental agency when you book your car rental.

Smart Strategy: Use a card that offers free CDW when you rent a car and save the money on the rental agency's coverage. Always check before traveling overseas to find out if you'll be able to take advantage of the CDW.

CHAPTER 13

Credit Card or Debit Card: The Great Debate

Having trouble getting approved for a credit card? Do you have bad credit? Maybe a debit card is the answer. Today, more and more banks and financial institutions are rushing to issue their customers debit cards. Two years ago, there were only 25 million debit cards in circulation. That number now exceeds 60 million and is climbing! According to the National Consumers League, by the year 2000, two-thirds of American households will have debit cards. This chapter will give you the facts you need to know about debit cards and how they differ from credit cards.

A credit card allows you to buy good and services now and pay later. You can spend up to a certain amount (your "credit limit"). The merchant or service provider from whom you made the purchase collects what you owe from the card issuer-the company that issued you the card. The card issuer then bills you on a monthly basis. The minimum monthly payment due is based on a percentage of your total balance. You, the cardholder, are charged interest on the unpaid balance you owe at the end of each period. (See more about credit cards in Chapter 12, "Plastic Power.")

A debit card is a combination of a credit card, check, and an automated teller machine ("ATM") card. There are two types of debit cards-online and off-line. Online debit cards are usually enhanced ATM cards. When you purchase something using an online debit card, you immediately electronically transfer money from your bank account to the merchant's bank account. You must punch in your personal identification number ("PIN") to access your account, an added security. Off-line debit cards may have the Visa or MasterCard ("MasterMoney") logo and can be used any place that accepts Visa or MasterCard credit cards. When you pay with an off-line debit card, you sign for your purchase without providing any additional identification, as with a credit card. The payment for the purchase is deducted from your checking account within one to three business days after the transaction. This "float" period is comparable to the time it takes for a regular check to clear the bank. Some debit cards handle both off-line and online debits, and you would choose the function you want when you use the card.

Most people use a credit or debit card for convenience. With both cards, you don't need to carry around a lot of cash when you are away from home. If an emergency arises, such as a broken-down car, and the cost of the repair outweighs the cash in your pocket, a credit or debit card especially comes in handy. Both credit and off-line debit cards are accepted nationwide and in foreign locations, and they save you from the identification hassles connected with writing a check.

The Major Differences Between Debit and Credit Cards

There are several major differences between credit and debit cards, outlined below.

Card Incentives

Certain credit cards will offer special services to make them more appealing, such as the replacement of lost or stolen merchandise, frequent flier programs, a warranty extension on a product, automatic air travel insurance, or collision waiver insurance for rental cars. Be sure to read the fine print on these benefits—they might not always be as wonderful as they sound. Debit cards, on the other hand, don't usually offer these kinds of services to the cardholder.

Fees/Costs

With debit cards, since the money comes directly from your checking account and you never have an outstanding balance, you avoid interest charges, late fees and over-limit fees that are connected to credit cards. If you take cash from your bank's ATM with your debit card, you don't pay interest or a transaction fee as you normally would when taking cash advances on a credit card. If you use a machine not associated with the bank that issued your ATM card, however, you may be hit with two separate fees-one from the bank you are using and another from your own bank for not using a machine on its network. You also may be charged a fee if you exceed your bank's quota of free debit transactions.

Spending Limit

A major disadvantage with credit cards is that an undisciplined cardholder can end up spending much more money than he or she can actually afford. A debit card avoids this problem because the funds are taken directly from your checking account. But this raises a different problem—if you spend more than you can afford with your debit card, checks you recently have written may bounce when they reach your bank. You will then have bounced-check fees to pay, which can be very high. Know how much money you have available in your account and budget carefully by tracking debit purchases in your check register. Also, be aware that a debit card may not give you a debit limit that is equal to the balance of the bank account to which it is linked. Check with your bank to find out your limit.

Credit Rating

Unlike credit cards, debit cards cannot help you build good credit because the accounts are not reported to credit bureaus. If you are looking to rebuild your credit and can't get a credit card, you should consider a secured card, where you place a deposit with the bank equal to your credit limit. Secured cards are a good way to build a strong credit history and as a bonus, the deposit you make will earn interest. Information on secured cards can be found on the Debt Counselors of America® website at www.GetOutOfDebt.org.

Billing Errors

Billing errors on credit card and debit card accounts are treated differently by federal laws. If you find an error on your credit card bill, you must notify the card issuer within 60 days of the day that the bill statement was sent. You should write a letter to the customer service department, give your name, account number, explanation of the error, amount involved, and attach any documents that show the error, such as a receipt showing the correct charge amount. Within 30 days, under federal law, a credit card issuer must either acknowledge receipt of your letter or correct the bill. If the card issuer does not correct the error within those 30 days, it must either do so within two billing cycles or explain why is hasn't. Until the dispute is resolved, you can withhold payment of the disputed amount and the card issuer cannot report you as delinquent to the credit bureaus. But the card issuer can apply that amount to your credit limit and can charge you interest on the disputed amount (and later subtract it if you are correct).

For debit cards, you also must notify the card issuer within 60 days of the date of the statement that shows the billing error (or the receipt). You should call the card issuer to notify it about the billing error, then immediately write a letter confirming the phone call. Under federal law, the card issuer has ten business days from the date of your notification to investigate the problem and correct any error. During its ten-day investigation, the card issuer does not need to credit your account with the amount in dispute. The card issuer can extend its investigation to 45 days, but only if it deposits the disputed amount into your account pending the result of the investigation.

Merchant Disputes

Different policies govern merchant disputes, depending on whether you used a credit or debit card. If you are dissatisfied with a product or service that you purchased using your credit card, the Fair Credit Billing Act gives you the same legal rights against the card issuer that you would have under your state laws against the merchant. So if your state law gives you the right to withhold payment to a merchant for defective merchandise or pay and later sue for a refund, you might also be able to withhold payment to your credit card issuer. State laws vary so you should talk to an attorney or to your local consumer affairs office. In general, your dispute rights only apply if you gave the merchant a chance to cure the problem, you bought the item in your home state or within 100 miles of your current mailing address, and the amount paid was more than $50.

There are no dispute rights for debit card purchases under federal laws. However, some debit card issuers treat disputes regarding the quality of goods or services the same whether a consumer uses credit or debit cards to make his purchases. Check the terms of your debit card agreement.

Theft Protection

Perhaps the most startling difference between debit and credit cards is the protection you get under federal law if your card is lost or stolen. If your debit card has been lost or stolen and you fail to notify your card issuer within a short period of time, there is very little protection for you under government regulations. Under government regulations, your liability is $0 for any unauthorized charges after you report the card missing, but you are liable for unauthorized charges made before you notified the card issuer in the following way. In general, you are responsible for $50 of any unauthorized withdrawals if you notify the card issuer within two business days after you realize the card is missing. You are responsible for $500 of any unauthorized withdrawals if you notify the card issuer after two business days after realizing the card is missing, but within 60 days after the card issuer mailed the bank statement listing the unauthorized withdrawals. If you fail to notify the card issuer within 60 days after your bank statement (with the unauthorized withdrawals) is mailed to you, you are responsible for all unauthorized withdrawals up to the time of your notification.

You may get relief outside of the federal regulations, thanks to consumer complaints. Visa and MasterCard, some banks, and some states have established policies that go beyond the federal law to protect consumers. Visa and MasterCard have policies that establish the same protections as exist for unauthorized credit card charges; debit card holders are not responsible for any unauthorized charges as long as they notify MasterCard or Visa immediately, and have a maximum liability of $50. Some banks and states also have capped the liability for unauthorized withdrawals on an ATM or debit card at $50. You should check with your financial institution and state Consumer Protection office about your liability limits.

Under government regulations, after you notify the debit card issuer about your lost or stolen debit card, the issuer has up to 20 days to credit your account for losses from unauthorized use of the card. Some debit card issuers promise faster provisional credit. Although they are not required to, as a measure of good customer service, some debit card issuers waive bounced check and other fees that incur from checks that unintentionally bounced because a debit card was stolen.

"I forgot my debit and credit cards.
Will you accept some of this antique paper money?"

A Few Final Suggestions

- If you are thinking about obtaining a financial transaction card to build your credit history, consider a secured card or credit card and use it responsibly.

- If you are having problems getting credit and don't have enough money to obtain a secured card, then a debit card may be the answer.

- For maximum consumer protection, a credit or secured card is preferable to a debit card.

- If you decide to get a debit card:

    1. Budget diligently and know how much money you have in your account. Write all withdrawals into your check register. Reconcile all ATM receipts with bank statements as soon as possible.

    2. Memorize your PIN and don't carry your PIN in your wallet, purse, or keep your PIN near your card. Never use your address, birthday, phone number or social security number as your PIN.

    3. Hold onto your receipts from your debit card transactions. A thief may get your name and debit card number from a receipt and order goods by mail or over the telephone.

    4. Check your debit card account statements to make sure there are no mistakes. If you lose your card or it is stolen, call your card issuer immediately and follow up the call with a confirmation letter.

    5. Avoid using your debit card for specific types of purchases. If you use a debit card to purchase airline, train, or bus tickets, the money is taken out of your checking account immediately or within three days after the reservation is made. If there is a change in your plans and you need to cancel or postpone your trip, it can take weeks to get a refund issued. Some major car rental companies do not accept debit cards for reservations.

    6. Think twice before linking your savings account to a checking account with debit card access. If a thief steals your card, both your checking and savings account can be drained. If you get an overdraft account that is linked to your checking account, you can get into even more trouble if your card is improperly used. Some card issuers or banks have daily limits on debit card withdrawals, which prevent thieves from clearing out bank accounts. Check with your debit card issuer to see if you have a daily limit.

Regardless of your decision, a debit, credit, or secured card will offer you the purchasing convenience you have been searching for. Please refer to the following table that compares credit and debit cards. Good luck!

Credit Card vs. Debit Cards
A Side-by-Side Comparison

CREDIT CARD	DEBIT CARD
Purchase Protection If you aren't satisfied with the quality of an item or service purchased, you have made an effort in good faith to resolve the dispute with the merchant and you haven't yet paid for the charge, you may have the right under your state's laws to withhold payment from your credit card issuer (must be for purchases greater than $50 made in your state or within 100 miles of your home). If you do dispute a payment, notify the issuer in writing.	*Purchase Protection* There is no dispute resolution process under federal regulations. However, the card issuer may offer the same dispute rights as with credit cards.
Billing Errors If there is an error on your credit card bill, you must write a letter to the credit card issuer, which must reach the issuer within 60 days after the first bill containing the error was mailed to you. The issuer must acknowledge the letter within 30 days after it is received or correct the bill within that amount of time. You can withhold the disputed amount until the dispute is resolved and the issuer cannot damage your credit rating.	*Billing Errors* If there is an error on account statement/receipt, notify the debit card issuer within 60 days after statement containing error was mailed to you. The issuer must investigate within 10 days. During this period, the issuer does not need to credit account with amount in dispute.
Grace Periods When you buy goods or services, you will not be charged interest on the purchase price until the due date or payment date on your next monthly statement.	*Grace Periods* When you buy goods or services, the funds come out of your checking account immediately or within 1 to 3 business days.
Fees/Costs - Usually charged on ATM withdrawals (interest and/or transaction fee) - No charge per purchase - Late fees - Over-the-limit fees.	*Fees/Costs* - No charges on ATM withdrawals at your own card issuer's branches (number of withdrawals may be limited depending on the issuer's policy). If you use a machine that is not associated with your debit card issuer, there may be a fee by issuer and the bank you are using. - May be a fee each time you make a purchase (can be charged by merchants or your card issuer; your issuer could also charge a monthly, quarterly, or yearly fee).

Credit Card vs. Debit Cards
A Side-by-Side Comparison (continued)

CREDIT CARD

Security
Requirement of your signature and the use of holograms and other technical devices (photos, personal identification codes) have made forgery very difficult.

Financial Management
Your statement can be used as a tool to provide a monthly spending record of purchases- allows you to keep track of how much you're spending, when and where you're spending it, and what you're spending it on.

Theft Protection
Immediate cancellation of account upon a phone call and with most cards, you will not be liable for fraudulent purchases made after the card is reported stolen (maximum liability of $50).

Building a Credit History
Your use of a credit card will be reported to the credit bureaus. This will allow you to either build a strong credit history or, if you are not careful and are unable to pay your debts, can lead to a bad credit rating.

DEBIT CARD

Security
PIN for online debit cards add security if lost or stolen. Only a signature is needed to use off-line debit cards.

Financial Management
A separate statement is not provided for debit card accounts. Consumers should keep accurate transaction records in their check registers.

Theft Protection
Under federal regulations, you are responsible for varying amounts depending on how long you wait to report that your card was lost or stolen. If you notify the card issuer within 2 business days, you are responsible for $50 AT MOST. If you notify the card issuer after 2 business days but within 60 days of receipt of the bank statement showing unauthorized transfers, you are responsible for $500 AT MOST. If you wait longer than 60 days, you are responsible for the total amount of unauthorized transfers. State laws and bank policies can set your liability at a lower amount or even 0, so be sure to read the disclosure forms that come with your debit card.

Building a Credit History
Unlike a credit card, your debit card will not be reported to the credit bureaus. It will not help build a credit history.

CHAPTER 14

Should You Lease Your Next Vehicle?

Searching for that perfect car or truck is not such an easy task anymore. Every auto dealer has a special deal just for you—and that deal is not all that easy to understand. Before you go shopping for your next vehicle, think about whether you want to lease or buy, and make sure you understand the mechanics of both options. What you are likely to find is that the decision to lease or buy your next vehicle comes down to what kind of person you are, and what habits you have.

An Up-Close Look at Leasing

Before you can make an informed decision to lease vehicle, you must know and understand the terms of the lease. Leasing includes terms that are not in the average consumer's vocabulary, so we will define them here in simpler terms.

When you lease a car, you will have a **negotiated vehicle price**, which is total price at which you agree to lease the car. You will put down a down payment up front when you sign the lease agreement and take possession of the vehicle. The amount that you agree to "finance," (i.e. the negotiated vehicle price plus any add-on features minus the down payment) is the **Adjusted Capitalized Cost**, or the **Net Cap Cost**.

To determine how much the lease will cost you each month, you need to know a host of other terms, including the residual value, the lease or rent charge, the money factor, the monthly lease rate, and the monthly depreciation.

The **Residual Value** is how much the auto will be worth at the end of your lease term.

The **Lease Charge**, or **Rent Charge**, is like the interest rate on a loan. The auto lessor charges you a monthly fee to lease the vehicle to you at the terms specified in the lease.

The **Money Factor** is the lease or rent charge divided by 24.

All of the above terms are used to calculate the **Monthly Lease Rate**, which in turn, makes up part of your monthly lease payment. The monthly lease rate is the Net Cap Cost plus the Residual Value, multiplied by the Money Factor.

EXAMPLE:

```
    $18,000   (Net Cap Cost)
+   $11,000   (Residual Value)
=   $29,000
x     .00333  (Money Factor-8% divided by 24)
=   $  96.57  (Monthly Lease Rate)
```

The **Monthly Depreciation** is also figured in your monthly lease payment. The monthly depreciation is the difference of the Net Cap Cost and Residual Value, divided by the term of the lease.

EXAMPLE:

```
    $18,000    (Net Cap Cost)
-   $11,000    (Residual Value)
=   $ 7,000
/ 36 months    (Term)
=   $194.44    (Monthly Depreciation)
```

Accordingly, your **Monthly Payment** will be the Monthly Lease Rate plus the Monthly Depreciation.

EXAMPLE:

```
    $ 96.57    (Monthly Lease Rate)
+   $194.44    (Monthly Depreciation)
=   $291.01    (Lease Payment)
```

The last few terms that you may encounter when leasing a vehicle are:

Security Deposit: your lease may contain a provision for a security deposit, which may be refundable if specified in the lease terms. This deposit is similar to a security deposit that a landlord would hold for a residence; if any damage occurs to the property that is specified in the lease, the lessor would be entitled to part or all of the security deposit.

An **Acquisition Fee** covers the administrative costs of the lessor, such as the cost of obtaining a credit report, verifying insurance coverage and processing the application and lease agreement.

If you understand and know the terms discussed above, you will be able to make an informed decision about whether you want to lease or buy a car.

An Up-Close Look at Buying

One of the most important things about buying a new car is understanding your financing options. There is a huge variety of financing options out there-there's your auto dealer's financing package, as well as those of your local bank, credit union and finance company. No matter whose financing package you take, you need to understand what kind of deal you are really getting-how much you are really paying and how much the vehicle is really worth.

The Loan-to-Value ratio is what most lenders use to determine how much to lend you. If your new car is valued at $20,000, a lender may insist that you have a loan-to-value ratio of 80%, or $16,000. You would have to make a $4,000 down payment, and the lender would agree to finance the rest.

One of the pitfalls of buying is that your car loses value when you drive it away. The value that your car loses over time is called depreciation. Different types of cars depreciate at different rates. A car that has a record of lasting longer than other cars on the road will probably have a slower depreciation rate and be worth more at any given time than a car with a reputation of being a "clunker."

The other big issue when buying a car is your interest rate, which varies widely among different lenders. Shop around and get the best rate before you agree to buy a vehicle so that you can make an informed decision, rather than being at the auto dealer's mercy to accept its financing package.

The Argument for Leasing

In general, leasing is good option for people who have little money in their pockets, can only make small monthly payments on a car, and for people who find that they buy a new car every three years or so.

Lower Down Payment

Leases traditionally require less money down than do comparable standards for purchasing a vehicle. If you are looking for a car with little or no money in your pocket, you could take advantage of some leases that advertise little or no money down.

Lower Monthly Payments

Monthly lease payments are usually lower than monthly loan payments for the same term.

If you buy a car every three years

Leasing is a great option for people who find that they buy a new car every three years or so. For example, if one consumer leases a car valued at $20,000, and obtains a new 36-month lease whenever the previous lease expires, he ends up spending $42,320 over a ten-year period. If that consumer chooses to buy the same vehicle every three years, using the old vehicle as a trade-in, gets financing for 36 months each time, and puts down a 20% down payment, he spends $64,512 over the same period. In this example, the consumer who buys the car spends 52% more than the person who leases the car. It should be noted that these values are estimates comparable to today's market. Accordingly, if you find that you buy a new car every three years or so, leasing may be a better option for you.

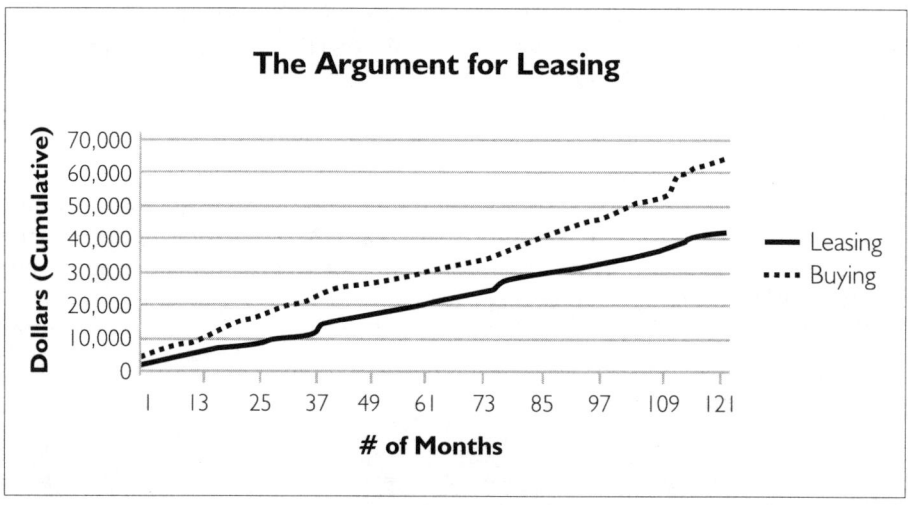

Leasing vs. Buying a Car
How do I decide?

WHEN YOU SHOULD LEASE

If you drive less than 12,000 miles/year. Many auto leases contain a provision that requires you to pay for each additional mile over a certain limit. That mileage limit is usually between 10,000 and 12,000 miles per year. If you usually drive less than that mileage limit, you will not occur these extra costs when leasing a vehicle.

If you plan to keep your vehicle for 3 years or less. Many auto lessors offer leases with terms of 24 and 36 months, and this can be an attractive feature to people who don't usually keep their car that long before they trade it in for a new one.

If you want lower payments and/or lower down payments. Leases usually contain lower down payments and have lower payments compared with auto loans of similar terms. This is due to the fact that an auto loan usually amortizes a larger portion of the car's value over the repayment period of the loan.

If you prefer newer vehicles. Leasing a car may save you some money if you usually trade in your car to buy another every few years. Leasing might be something you should consider if you think having a car payment is just a fact of life and you plan to continue the trend of purchasing a new car every few years.

If you keep your car well maintained. A usual provision in an auto lease is that you agree to keep the car well maintained and in good running order. If you are lousy at doing that, it will cost you at the end of the lease; the car will probably not be worth its residual value and you will be required to make up the difference.

WHEN YOU SHOULD BUY

If you drive more than 12,000 miles/year. If you drive more than the annual mileage limit required by the lease, you may want to compare the cost of buying the car to the estimated total leasing cost. If you drive a lot of miles over the mileage limit, you will probably be better off financially buying the auto.

If you plan to keep your vehicle for 3 years or more. If you usually keep a car or truck for a longer period of time than what is offered by the lease, compare the cost of buying the vehicle at the end of the lease to buying the auto now instead of leasing it. In many instances, if you plan to purchase the auto at the end of the lease, buying can make more sense financially.

If you like the idea of owning your car. Auto leasing is most comparable to "renting" your car. If you don't like the idea of renting your car, and it is important to you that your car is yours, then you are probably a good candidate for auto ownership.

If you like the idea of eventually paying off your car. Being debt free is always a good dream to have, and being without a car payment can be a reality if you buy instead of lease. Many leases do, however, contain purchase options to buy the car once the lease expires. By that time, though, you have already put a lot of money into a lease that could have been used to purchase the car in the first place.

If you like the customized look. If customizing your new car is what you had in mind, you definitely should consider buying. Changing the appearance of a leased vehicle alters the value, and this may prove to be costly at the termination of the lease.

If you don't need to take advantage of the advantages of a car lease, i.e. the lower down payment, lower monthly payments, and if you don't buy a new car every three years, then it is a better financial decision to buy a vehicle.

If you buy and keep a vehicle, you would eventually pay off your car loan. You could save those extra funds that you were paying monthly on the car loan for emergencies, a child's education, your retirement, or even to pay for your next car in cash. We illustrate the advantage of buying in the graph below. In the graph, we depict three consumers. One buys a car valued $20,000 with 36-month financing at 8.5%. Once this consumer pays off his loan, he deposits the monthly car payment amount into a mutual fund that follows the Standard & Poor's 500 index (which has averaged approximately 15% over the last 10 years).

The second consumer leases the same car for 36 months. He pays a $1,000 down payment, with $850 due in acquisition and title fees. This consumer then exercises a purchase option on the lease for 36 months. When he pays off the loan, he also deposits the same amount as the first consumer into the same mutual fund.

The third consumer leases a new vehicle every three years without exercising any option to purchase. All leases have the same terms as described for the second consumer, and all three cars have the same value.

In this example, the first consumer (the buyer) amasses $74,300 over a ten-year period. The second consumer (who leased, and then bought) saves $34,940 over the same period. The third consumer (who continued leasing) spends a total of $42,320 in this amount of time.

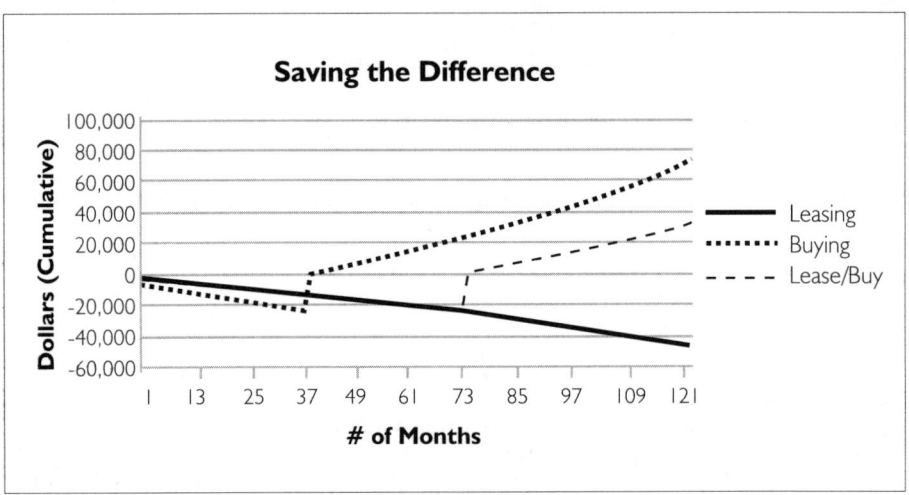

Shopping for the Best Deal

Whether you decide to lease or buy a vehicle, be smart while looking. Here are some tips on how to get the best deal you can.

Shop 'til you drop.

Shop around before negotiating so that you know (1) what price other car dealers want for the same vehicle (use pricing guides or services to see the invoice prices for the vehicle; don't just look at the retail sticker on the car); and (2) what financing terms are available for leases or auto loans. You don't have to sign a lease, loan or purchase agreement on your first visit; don't let a salesperson pressure you if you aren't ready to make a final decision. Ask the dealer to explain anything that you don't understand. Also, don't fill out a lease application until you are ready to sign the final documents. Each application you complete may generate an inquiry on your credit report. Many lenders and lessors view too many credit inquiries as a negative factor when evaluating your credit profile.

Negotiate the best price.

The price you negotiate on any vehicle is the starting point in determining the cost of leasing or buying your car. Have a maximum price that you want to spend for a car. Don't let the dealer talk you into a price that doesn't fit in your spending plan.

Tell the dealer whether you intend to lease or buy.

This can save you lots of time.

Get the proper value for your trade-in.

If you are trading in your current vehicle, get an estimate of its value from a used car dealer or financial institution before visiting the auto dealer.

If you decide to lease, ask about gap insurance.

Gap insurance is insurance that will protect you against any "gap" in coverage between the value of the vehicle when you return it and the residual value as stated in the contract. This coverage may also provide provisions regarding theft or accidents. This is especially useful coverage in open-end leases (leases where you can be held liable for any difference in value). In closed-end leases, you may still be liable for this difference; read the lease agreement carefully to find out exactly what your liability would be upon lease termination.

Know your early termination options in a lease agreement.

Find out when you are allowed to terminate your lease, if at all, and how much it will cost you. This simple question can stop future headaches if for some reason you need to get out of your lease agreement.

Only lease for a term that is within the manufacturer's warranty period.

This will save you from paying for repairs for damages that occur to a leased vehicle after the manufacturer's warranty expires.

Consider leasing a vehicle that has a high residual value.

The higher the residual value, the lower the cost of the lease may be; however, any purchase options contained in the lease will probably have a higher price tag. Vehicles that last longer are the most likely candidates for having higher residual values. Check with a consumer reporting agency to find out which cars retain their value the longest.

When Your Lease Is Over

Once the term of your lease has expired, you have a choice to make. Here are the options that are usually available:

Return the car to the dealer.

If you don't plan to lease another car, or want to negotiate with another dealer, you can simply return the vehicle to the dealer. There may be charges at lease-end, like a termination fee, excessive mileage charges or charges for excessive wear and tear.

Purchase the vehicle.

The lease may contain a provision to purchase the vehicle at lease-end, with the purchase price usually being set at the residual value. If you have taken good care of the car, it may be worth more than the residual value, making this option a good deal for you. If the car is in bad shape, compare the cost of turning in the car to buying the vehicle.

Negotiate a new deal with the dealer.

If the car is worth more than the residual value, use the equity in the car to negotiate a lease on another car. You always have the option to lease another car, but you may not always have the extra value, greater than the residual value. Use this to your advantage if you find yourself fortunate enough to have this benefit.

Sell the car and pay off the residual value.

If the lease has an option to purchase, as many leases do, and if the car is in good condition, then you could exercise the option to purchase first, and then sell the car yourself. This could be beneficial if the car has held its value well and the residual value is less than the price for which you could sell it.

When You Can't Make Your Lease Payments

Everybody has good intentions when entering a lease agreement, but financial hardships can befall even those with the best intentions. If you can no longer afford to make your lease payments due to such a hardship, consider the following:

Ask the auto lessor for your options under your lease for early termination.

It is usually wise to be up front and honest with your auto lessor, and to let him know about your hardship. The lessor may be able to offer you other options that will help you.

Ask the auto lessor if you can sell the car to pay off the lease.

If the car is in good condition, you may be able to advertise the vehicle at a price that would pay the termination costs of the lease. Ask your lessor how much the termination cost would be, and make sure you ask the lessor if this option is available before you sell the car.

Ask the auto lessor about a substitution of the leased vehicle.

If you just can't afford the auto you have leased but are able and willing to lease a car of a lesser value, ask the auto lessor about substituting the auto you have for another auto that will produce a lower lease payment. In some instances, your auto lessor may be willing to do this only if you terminate your current lease and apply for another one.

Ask the auto lessor what the total cost would be to return the car before the lease termination date.

Obviously, there will be some kind of charge associated with this. However, these charges may be less than trying to make your remaining lease payments.

Ask the auto lessor about an extension of the lease or deferment of the lease payment.

The auto lessor may be willing to renegotiate the lease over a longer period of time to lower your payment amount. In a few cases, your auto lessor may agree to defer your lease payment; this would depend entirely on your situation and the willingness of the lessor to work with you.

Find out if your lease is assumable.

If your auto lease contains an assumption clause, you may be able to find someone who would be willing to assume, or take over, the payments on your auto lease.

CHAPTER 15

How to Buy a Car With Marks on Your Credit

If you have any negative marks on your credit—such as a late payment, default, repossession, foreclosure, lien, judgment or bankruptcy—you probably think you'll have a hard time buying a car (or truck or van). Think again. There are many options available to you, but you've got to understand the advantages and disadvantages of each.

Consider the following:

- You can buy a car using the dealer's financing.
- You can buy a car using an alternative source of financing.
- You can pay cash for a car.
- You can lease a car.

Before You Start Looking

Unless you plan to pay cash for your vehicle, get your ducks lined up before you go shopping-for either the vehicle or your loan. If you have poor credit, you will want to have on hand the following:

- A copy of a recent pay stub.
- A statement from your employer verifying your employment and income.
- The names and addresses of your creditors and your account numbers, including your mortgage lender, student loan holder and credit card issuers.

- The bank name, bank address, and the account numbers of your checking, savings and money market accounts.
- A copy of your credit report. Be sure you know what's in your credit report, as anyone to whom you apply for financing will pull a copy.

Also, take some time to figure out how much you can afford to pay each month. Total up your monthly expenses—including your rent or mortgage, utilities, food, clothing, transportation, education, insurance, taxes, loans—and subtract that number from your monthly income. What's left over is the maximum you have to put toward monthly car payments. Aim for payments of at least 20% less, however, to give yourself a cushion.

Buy a Car Using the Dealer's Financing

Most people want to be able to walk into a showroom, pick out a car, sign a few papers in the back and drive away. But does "most people" include the folks with bad credit? And even if it does, is that the best way to go about buying a car?

Maybe. Car dealers want to move the vehicles on their lots to make room for new ones so they advertise heavily. Open a newspaper or turn on a television and you'll see ads screaming low financing, such as 1.9%. These ads are often aimed at people with low income or poor credit who can't afford high-priced deals, and probably sound like a bargain, especially if you are paying 20% on a credit card. But ironically, low financing doesn't always come cheap. Before applying for a low-rate loan, answer the following questions:

- Are you being charged a higher price to qualify for the low rate than you would be charged if you paid cash or used an alternative financing source?
- Are you required to make a larger-than-usual down payment, such as 25% or 30%? This is often required of a person with poor credit.
- Will you be required to make a balloon payment—possibly for several thousands of dollars—at the end of the loan period?
- Is the loan limited to a set number of months, such as 24 or 36? Many more traditional car loans give you up to 60 months to pay for the vehicle.
- Must you buy special services or merchandise, such as an extended warranty, credit insurance or rust-proofing, to qualify for the loan?

If the loan smells bad, ask the dealer about more traditional financing at a higher rate but with fewer restrictions. Because of your credit history, you may be required to make a larger-than-usual down payment, or you may be asked to provide a cosigner, a person who agrees to make the payments if you default. If you go with dealer financing, read the contract carefully. Make sure you understand all terms and that they reflect the agreement you made with the dealer. Don't sign if you don't understand or agree with any item in the contract.

Buy a New Car Using Alternative Financing

A car dealer may lead you to believe that he's your only source of financing. Nonsense. All financial institutions (banks, savings and loans, and credit unions) make car loans. While these loans aren't as low as the low-rate dealer financing loans, especially for used cars, they don't have the hidden charges. If you have a long-term relationship with one particular financial institution, consider applying there first. If you've never bounced checks or defaulted on a loan, you might be pleasantly surprised that you qualify for a loan, even with marks on your credit report. Alternatively, the financial institution may require a large down payment or a co-signer. If you can't afford the large down payment or don't want to use a co-signer, try proposing that either:

- The interest rate begin at a point higher than the financial institution initially offers you, if the institution agrees to reduce it to that rate after you make six consecutive payments (this will allow you to demonstrate your credit worthiness to them.); or

- You will maintain a minimum balance in a savings account that the institution can use as a setoff—that is, to take money from the account to apply toward the amount of any missed loan payments.

Another alternative source of financing doesn't involve a financial institution; consider friends or relatives.

Propose a written business deal. Ask to borrow the money at a rate less than you'd pay a bank but more than your friend would earn on her money in a savings or money market account. For example, if the bank would charge you 7%, but would pay your friend Mavis only 3% on her savings deposit, ask Mavis to lend you the money to buy the car, and offer to pay her 5%—a deal for you both.

Pay Cash for a Car

If your credit is very bad, you can't afford a large down payment, you don't have a co-signer, or no one will give you a loan for any other (non-discriminatory) reason, you will have to change your expectations if you want to buy a car. You need to save up money to pay cash. This will require discipline.

Your first step will be to trim your expenses as much as possible so that you'll have a little bit left over each month to put aside. To get a handle on where your money goes, take a month to make lists of every outlay of cash or cash equivalent, such as check or ATM card, used to make purchases. At the end of the month, look carefully at your lists. Chances are you'll find places where you are spending money unnecessarily. For example, bringing your lunch to work rather than going out, even going out cheap, will save you a bundle each week. So will using the public library to read the daily paper or to take out books, CDs and videos instead of buying or renting. Look for other ways to save.

Your second step is to look for things around the house you can sell, such as sports equipment, electronics, large appliances and anything else that's just taking up space. Let your friends and co-workers know what you have, hold a garage sale or run an ad in the local freebie paper.

Granted, raising money to pay cash may not be your first or even second choice in buying a car, but it will teach you discipline. And you can use the same technique to save up your money so that you can apply for a secured credit card and begin to rebuild your credit. And imagine how it will help you when you go to raise money to buy a house.

Lease a Car

The number of people leasing cars has skyrocketed for a very good reason: leases can seem cheap. Lease agreements usually require a low or no down payment, and lease payments are usually lower than loan payments for the same vehicle. This means that people with poor credit may have an easier time qualifying for a lease than for a loan. But leasing is rarely a good option. First, you don't own the car. You are paying to drive someone else's vehicle. If you want to own a car at the lease end, you will have the pay a bundle for it—far more than the vehicle is worth. Your alternative is to enter into a new lease for a different vehicle, meaning that you make perpetual car payments.

If you're still lured into a lease, read the fine print carefully. Be sure you understand all of the following:

- Whether the lease is open-end or closed-end. In an open-end lease, you must pay the difference between the value stated in your contract and the vehicle's appraised value when you return the vehicle. A close-end lease allows you to walk away, but you may be responsible for certain charges.

- Closed-end lease charges, such as excess mileage (you're usually limited to 12,000 to 15,000 a year), abnormal wear and tear (is a ding normal or not?) and the disposition of the vehicle.

- The price if you were to exercise your option to purchase the car either at the lease end or earlier.

- Lease inception fees, such as a low down payment, security deposit, acquisition fee, first month's payment, taxes and title fees.

- Charges for terminating the lease early. These are usually very high and often hard to understand, based on a complex formula. Be sure you know exactly how the fee for terminating the lease early is calculated.

- The warranty coverage—it should cover the entire lease term and the number of miles you're likely to drive.

- The availability of gap insurance to cover the difference between what you owe under the lease agreement and what the car is worth if it's stolen or totaled in an accident. The difference can be many thousands of dollars.

So, what are the lessons here? First, don't assume that the marks on your credit report will keep you from getting a new car. Second, do your homework in advance so you can present yourself in the best possible light and be upfront about your problems. Third, shop around. Remember that car dealers are in the business of selling and lenders are in the business of making loans. They don't make money by saying no. And finally, beware of deals that seem too good to be true. Read the fine print. If the offer is questionable, pass it up.

"I assure you. The repo-man will NEVER look out here!"

CHAPTER 16

When You Can't Make Your Car Payments

If you find yourself unable to make your car (car is shorthand for any motor vehicle) payments, you'll want to act quickly. In most states, if you miss a payment, whether you have bought or leased the vehicle, the dealer or lender has the right to repossess it almost immediately. Here are some strategies to consider when your car payments become too much, including what to do if your car is repossessed.

Negotiating with the Dealer or Lender

If you've missed a payment but the dealer or lender hasn't repossessed the car or declared you in default, or if you're current on your payments but know you won't be able to make them for a couple of months, call the dealer or lender and ask if it's possible to get an extension of your agreement. An extension lets you skip a few payments now and have the skipped and any missed payments tacked on at the end of the agreement. Usually, to get an extension, the following must be true:

- your purchase or lease agreement is not considered in default
- you have made at least six payments under your agreement, and
- you agree to pay a fee for the extension. Fees vary among the various lenders and dealers: you may be charged a flat fee (such as $50), you may be charged a percentage (often around 1%) of the outstanding balance or you may be required to pay up to one month's worth of interest.

If the dealer or lender is not willing to grant you an extension, he may rewrite the agreement to reduce your monthly payments. Occasionally, you can get a reduction in the interest rate. More often, however, you are simply given a longer time to pay what you owe. This will increase the total interest you will pay.

Getting Out of Your Purchase Agreement

If your agreement is for the purchase of the car, as opposed to leasing it, and you know you won't be able to make your payments for several months, your best bet is to try to get out of the agreement. There are two ways you can accomplish this. One is to sell the car on your own. This is a good idea. The other is to give the car back to the lender-a sort of voluntary repossession. This is not a good idea.

Selling on Your Own

When you sell a car without having the title or "pink slip" (the motor vehicle department keeps the pink slip until the car is paid for in full), you will have to get the lender to sign off on the sale. If the car is in good condition, you can probably get top dollar for it—at least the top dollar that the car is worth. If the sales amount doesn't cover the total amount you still owe the lender, you may have to come up with the difference before the lender agrees to the deal. If you're flat broke, out of work and lacking in any assets, the lender may sign off and waive the balance owed.

Giving the Car Back

If you're inclined to just give the car back to the lender, think again. Giving the car back doesn't end your obligation. The lender sells the car at an auction where mostly used car dealers attend, who have a motive to keep the bids very low. Cars rarely bring in even half of what they are worth. The difference between what you still owed the lender when you returned the car and the amount brought in at the auction is called a deficiency. It's usually several thousands of dollars. And you are liable for it.

Getting Out of Your Lease

Over one-third of new car owners lease, rather than purchase, their vehicles. Although leasing isn't for everyone, some people swear by it for three reasons:

- Lease payments are lower than loan payments for the same car.

- Leasing gives you the chance to drive a more expensive car than you could afford to buy.

- If you like to drive a new car every few years, you will pay much less by leasing than by buying.

But leasing has serious disadvantages.

First, if you continually lease your cars, you will have never-ending car payments. Second, if you decide to buy the car at the lease-end, you'll pay several thousands of dollars more than if you had bought initially. Third, most leases charge you as much as $0.25 a mile if you exceed the annual limit, usually between 12,000 and 15,000 miles. If you do extensive driving, you shouldn't lease.

Fourth, not all leasing costs are disclosed up front. While a federal law called the Consumer Leasing Act requires lease agreements to include a statement of costs, many lease agreements are ambiguously drafted with key provisions buried in the fine print. And the law does not obligate a dealer to disclose the interest rate that's been built into your payments. To find out the interest rate on a lease, you will have to ask the dealer for something called the leasing factor. Multiply that factor by 24 and you'll get the approximate interest rate.

Fifth, getting out of your lease can cost you a bundle. If you want to cancel your lease, look carefully at the provision describing what happens if you default or want to terminate the lease early. The provision probably states that you'll owe an amount of money based on a given formula. If you were to calculate the sum, you'd find that it was several thousands of dollars. It's really nothing other than a penalty for breaking your agreement with the dealer.

The Consumer Leasing Act gives you the right to cancel the lease if the termination formula is so complex that you can't easily figure out how much you owe. But this will be hard for you to assert with success. Lawyers for car manufacturers have rewritten lease contracts to avoid most of the ambiguities because of successful consumer lawsuits. You may not like the amount you come up with, but it shouldn't be all that hard to figure out what the amount is.

But maybe the dealer used an old lease agreement or added some terminology making the termination formula too complicated for you to figure out what you owe. In that case, write to the dealer stating that you want to terminate the lease early. State further that the termination provision of the lease agreement is ambiguous and that you know you are entitled to sue for damages because of the dealer's failure to use a reasonable formula. Finally, state that you are willing to waive your right to sue for those damages if the dealer will waive the balance you owe. It's unlikely that the dealer would concede 100% of the early termination penalty, but he may be willing to negotiate with you to reduce the amount you must pay or at least to let you pay if off over time.

Another way some dealers have let people out of their lease is to find someone to take over your lease for you. However, the new person will have to be approved by the dealer first.

If the Vehicle Is Repossessed

In most states, your car can be taken one minute after midnight the day after your payment was due—without any warning. In about a dozen states, the dealer or lender must send you notice that you are in default of your loan or lease agreement and give you a very short period of time to make up the missed payments before grabbing your car.

Despite what you might have seen at the movies (remember the cult film, *Repo Man?*) laws do regulate how car repossessions are to take place. A repo man can't use force, although he can use a duplicate key or hotwire your car. Furthermore, he can take your car from your carport or unlocked garage. It's illegal to break into a locked garage. The repo man knows that people avoiding repossession tend to park their cars within about three to five blocks from their home. Repo men find cars quickly.

Once your car is taken, you usually will have a very short period of time to redeem it—that is, get it back by paying the entire balance due. The lender or dealer may let you redeem the vehicle by reinstating the original contract, as long as you make up the missed payments and late fees, and the cost of the repossession and storage.

The lender or dealer probably will not let you reinstate the contract if any of the following are true:

- You've had the agreement reinstated in the past
- You lied on your credit application
- You hid the property to try and avoid the repossession
- You haven't taken good care of the vehicle, or
- You were violent with the repo man.

The lender or dealer must send you a notice of your right to redeem the car. If you don't redeem it in the allowed time, the lender or dealer will sell it at a used car auction, where it will bring in maybe one-third or one-half of its value. You're liable for the deficiency—the difference between what you still owe and what the car sells for—unless you can prove any of the following (often as a defense in a lawsuit where the lender or dealer sues you for the deficiency):

- The lender or dealer routinely accepted late payments from you and then repossessed without warning.
- You were not told of your right to redeem.
- You weren't told of the date and place of the auction sale.
- The sale wasn't conducted in a "commercially reasonable" manner. No one really knows what this means and courts virtually always rule that auction sales of repossessed cars were done in a reasonable manner for that industry.

If your vehicle is repossessed, do what you can to redeem, if for no other reason than to sell it yourself and avoid the deficiency. If you wind up owing a deficiency, try negotiating for a reduction of the amount or an agreement to pay it off over time.

CHAPTER 17

Repossession: Why It Happens, What You Can Do, and Your Rights Before, During and After

If you fail to make payments on a car loan, or anticipate a problem paying in the near future, you should be familiar with the process of repossession and what rights you may have. This chapter will cover your rights before and after repossession, starting with the security agreement you signed when you bought the car and ending with your rights after a creditor sale of your car. Specifically, this chapter will answer the following:

- How does the creditor have a security interest in your car and what does this mean?
- How can you default on a loan?
- When can you reinstate the contract or redeem the car?
- Do you have rights to be notified before repossession?
- How can you stop self-help repossession?
- What are your rights before and after the sale of your vehicle?

It is important to know that every state has a different mix of laws on this subject, and the rights discussed in this chapter may or may not be available in your particular state. You must check with an attorney in your state to see which of these rights is available to you.

Did the Consumer Sign a Valid Written Security Agreement?

A car can only be repossessed by the lender that specifically took the car as collateral. Another of your creditors cannot repossess your car unless you have a security agreement that specifically states that your car is collateral for that loan. For example, if you are delinquent on regular credit card debt, the credit card company cannot repossess your car to collect the credit card debt.

When a consumer buys a car and pays with a car loan, he signs a security agreement. For the agreement to be valid, the consumer must have signed it, it must describe the type of "collateral" (the car) and the value given, and the consumer must have "rights to the collateral." A consumer has rights to the collateral if the car belongs to that consumer, not to someone else. Accordingly, if a parent buys a car for her daughter, the daughter, who possesses the car and has all rights to the collateral, must sign the security agreement. If the daughter does not sign the agreement, there is no valid security interest and the creditor may not be able to repossess the car.

It is important to check the agreement to see if there are any mistakes or omissions. If there is a mistake in the security agreement that makes the agreement invalid, the creditor cannot repossess the car, even if you defaulted on the loan. You should have received a copy of the agreement at the time you bought the car, but if you no longer have a copy of your security agreement, you can ask your creditor for a copy. Although you may not have a legal right to another copy of the agreement, you should contact your local attorney general or consumer affairs office if you believe there may be a problem with the agreement and your creditor won't give you a copy.

Did the Consumer Default on the Loan?

Before a lender can repossess your car, you must default on the loan. The usual way that a consumer defaults on a loan is by failing to make a monthly installment payment. (If you are in this situation or close to it, see Chapter 16, "When You Can't Make Your Car Payments.") But there are other ways that you can default, and these ways are spelled out in the security agreement that you signed when you bought the car. Some examples include: failing to purchase insurance, losing or destroying the car, selling the car, or moving the car to another location without the lender's permission. If you don't understand why or how you defaulted, you should look at your agreement to see what constitutes a default.

There are occasions where you may default under the agreement but your creditor still cannot repossess your car. Many states find that if the creditor has accepted late payments from you before, the creditor cannot then declare that you defaulted without giving you reasonable notice. In other words, the creditor would have to tell you that he would consider all future late payments as your defaulting on the loan.

In addition, there can be no default if the underlying obligation is extinguished (you paid off the loan), the contract is voided under the laws of your state, or if you notified the creditor that you are withholding payments because of the creditor's breach of warranty. You should check your state laws for additional rights since your state laws may further restrict the grounds for default.

Did the Loan Accelerate?

Assuming you defaulted on your loan by not paying on the loan, it is important that you know whether or not your security agreement with the creditor has an "acceleration clause." Once a loan has accelerated, you can no longer "cure" the default by just paying the past due amount. Instead, the lender can demand the entire balance of the loan due or repossess the vehicle. Your state law determines whether or not your creditor must warn you beforehand that your loan will accelerate and whether or not your creditor must tell you that you have a "right to cure" the default.

The first thing you should do is check your security agreement to see if there is an acceleration clause. A loan will only accelerate if there is an acceleration clause between the debtor and the lender. If there is no acceleration clause in the agreement, the creditor can only demand that you pay the past due amount. The acceleration clause must be clear in the agreement and state that if the consumer meets one of the grounds for acceleration as defined in the agreement, the creditor may accelerate the debt. Grounds for acceleration can include such things as: your commencement of bankruptcy proceedings, your refusal to allow the creditor to inspect the car, or your default on the loan, as defined in the agreement.

Upon acceleration, the full loan amount would become due immediately. It is unlikely that a consumer can come up with that sum in a short period of time, and acceleration almost always results in default on the total balance of the loan. At that time, the lender can repossess and sell the car to recover the total remaining loan balance.

The creditor can even accelerate "at will" if he truly believes that your prospect for payment is impaired. For instance, if the creditor believes that the car has been abandoned, the creditor can accelerate at will to recover the total amount owed. Before a creditor can do this, he must perceive a deterioration of the consumer's financial condition since the loan was made. Check your agreement for a provision allowing acceleration at will.

Did the Consumer Get Notice of Acceleration and the Right to Cure?

Under the terms of your agreement, the creditor may not have to tell you that your loan is accelerating. Most agreements have a provision waiving the consumer's right to notice of acceleration. Accordingly, a creditor can demand that you pay the full amount of the loan and could repossess the car without ever notifying you. Check your agreement. If there is no waiver, the creditor must notify you after default to tell you that the loan will accelerate, and give you a reasonable opportunity to pay the defaulted amount before acceleration.

Even if you waived notice of acceleration in the agreement, you still may get some help from your state laws. Some state laws—usually called "right to cure" laws—require notice before acceleration, and these laws override the waiver provisions of your agreement. Under a right to cure law, the creditor must allow the consumer to pay back payments plus delinquent charges, and reinstate the loan within a particular amount of time before the note will accelerate. This means that your creditor would have to give you notice before acceleration AND give you the chance to correct the situation.

If your state does not have a right to cure law and you waived your right to notice in your security agreement, your creditor still may have to tell you about your right to cure the default. The waiver may not stand if there is any inconsistency about a right to notice in other provisions of the agreement. For instance, the waiver would be invalid if there are provisions in your agreement that mention "on demand," implying that you have the right to notice of a right to cure.

State laws may further restrict grounds for default and acceleration, and may specify the number of times that you may have the right to cure.

Was the Creditor's Self-Help Repossession Lawful?

If there was a valid security interest, you defaulted on the loan, and the loan accelerated, you risk creditor repossession. In most states, a lender can seize a car without first having to go to court. This is called "self-help repossession." Creditors must comply with many technical requirements to repossess your car by self-help. Some state requirements that may protect you against self-help repossession include:

- **Express consent.** Some states do not permit repossession without the consumer's express consent (usually in the signed agreement). You consent if you specifically knew of the creditor's right to repossession and specifically knew that the creditor could repossess your car without having to go to court first.

- **Military personnel or dependents.** If you are in the military or are a dependent, you are protected by the federal Soldiers' and Sailors' Civil Relief Act. This law, however, provides only temporary and partial relief. If you bought a car before you entered the military service and default on your car payment while in the military, your creditor must take you to court to repossess the car. However, your creditor can still use self-help repossession to repossess a car that you bought while you were in the military. But you still may be protected in another way: standard military policy requires that any repossessor entering a base must be accompanied by military police. If you are present during a self-help repossession, a court may find that the presence of a military official forced you to consent to repossession, which is wrongful repossession.

- **Native Americans.** Native Americans may be protected if tribal law prohibits self-help repossession.

Did the Creditor Breach the Peace During Self-Help Repossession?

A creditor cannot breach the peace when he repossesses a car. Breaching the peace includes many situations, such as:

- Touching or pushing you.

- Damaging your property during repossession.

- **Tricking or lying to you, in some states.** A few courts have held that laws cannot encourage lying and trickery to repossess collateral. Courts are divided as to whether a repossessor can trick you to take your car. In one instance, a creditor breached the peace when he pulled the debtor's car to the side of the road, rode back with the debtor to the dealership, and seized the car while the debtor was inside. In another case, a creditor breached the peace when he lied and said he was a government official. However, some courts have found that there was no wrongful repossession when the creditor lied and said he was taking the car for repairs.

- **Threatening you if you feel immediate fear.** For example, a creditor's threat to seize your car at some future time does not put you in immediate fear so there is no breach of peace.

- **Ignoring your objections.** If you, your relative, or your friend objects to the repossession but the creditor still repossesses the car, he breaches the peace. You should object at the time the creditor takes the car. If you object after the creditor took the car, it is too late. If a sheriff or other government official is present, don't resist his seizure of the car, but verify the official's authenticity.

- **Entering a closed garage.** Even without physically breaking in, a creditor breaches the peace when he enters a closed garage. Generally, there is no breach of peace if the creditor takes the vehicle from the public street, a parking lot, a private driveway, an open garage or a carport. A creditor's trespass can be a breach if there is a potential for immediate violence.

- **Police presence.** If the creditor brings a police officer not through a paper of the court and the presence of the officer so intimidates the debtor as to have "forced" him to consent to repossession, the creditor breached the peace.

Your state laws may further limit who can engage in self-help repossession. For example, a state law may permit self-help repossession by licensed personnel, employees of the creditor or automobile dealers only.

If your creditor wrongfully repossesses your car or breaches the peace, depending on your state and its laws, the court may not allow the creditor to keep the car or to collect a deficiency, may stop the subsequent creditor sale of your car, and may force the creditor to pay you for the market value of the vehicle at the time of seizure, or pay for damages for your loss of use, mental anguish, or inconvenience. You could also be reimbursed for attorneys' fees.

Note: Unsecured Property Repossessed with the Car. Cellular phones, stereos, and other items attached to the consumer's car can be repossessed only if the security agreement specifically covers these items. The creditor must return personal property and is liable for the consumer's loss of use of property or any damages to property while in the creditor's custody. If your creditor seized unsecured property with the car, you should inventory the missing property and demand its return. If your creditor refuses, you can sue the creditor for the property's value, for your loss of use or for any damages to the property while it was in the creditor's custody.

Did the Creditor Properly Dispose of the Car After Repossession?

After repossession, there are six possible ways that the creditor can dispose of your car.

- **Reinstatement.** After repossession, your state law may give you the right to reinstate the contract by paying the amount past due. If this is the case, the creditor must give you notice of your right to reinstate and the amount due. You have a particular time period, usually 15 days following repossession, to reinstate the contract. You may only get one opportunity to reinstate a contract. If the creditor does not comply with reinstatement procedures, he may be barred from later obtaining a deficiency judgment and may even owe you money.

- **Redemption.** Every state gives you a chance to redeem your car by paying off the entire loan plus reasonable repossession and storage charges at any time before your creditor sells or otherwise disposes of the car, even if you had voluntarily surrendered the car. A written waiver of the right to redeem is ineffective unless you signed a written waiver AFTER you defaulted on the loan. Unfortunately, this right to redeem does not help most consumers who have their cars repossessed due to money troubles, and cannot come up with a large lump sum of money. Before you redeem, you should know the loan amount, repossession fees, costs associated with the sale, and reasonable attorneys' fees and legal expenses. If the debt has accelerated, the creditor is not entitled to unearned interest or insurance payments that are not owed because the note has been paid off early.

    Remember: you may be better off buying your car at the repossession sale than redeeming. The sale price at a creditor sale may be less than the amount you owe. However, you still will be liable for the amount of your loan obligation and repossession costs that are more than the sale price of the car (the deficiency).

- **Strict Foreclosure.** Your creditor could keep your car in satisfaction of your obligation, which is called "strict foreclosure." If your creditor elects strict foreclosure, you would not owe the creditor any payments, although your creditor can keep all prior amounts that you paid. If the creditor intends to elect strict foreclosure, he must tell you in writing. You can object to strict foreclosure in writing within a certain amount of time depending on your state, usually within 21 days of the notice. You should object to strict foreclosure if you believe that you or the creditor could get a sale price that would cover the remaining amount that you owe plus any repossession, reconditioning and sale costs.

If your creditor has repossessed your car but has not disposed of it in any way, it may no longer be worthwhile to sell the car. You can argue that the creditor, in effect, elected strict foreclosure because his holding onto your car for so long made a subsequent sale commercially unreasonable. This is called "constructive strict foreclosure." If you successfully argue constructive strict foreclosure, your creditor would not have a claim to any deficiency. Even if you live in a state that does not have laws on constructive strict foreclosure, many courts will treat the creditor's repossession without disposition as extinguishing the debt for the value of the car taken. (See "delay of sale" under the discussion of Creditor Sale).

If you have paid at least 60% toward the car, your creditor cannot elect strict foreclosure.

- **Judicial Sale.** A creditor could dispose of your car though judicial sale. A creditor will rarely do this since it adds extra court costs and a creditor generally can sell the car without having to go to court first.

- **Consumer Sale.** Your creditor may permit you to sell the car. You should take advantage of this if you believe that you can get a better price on your own. In fact, it may be unreasonable for a creditor NOT to let you sell the car if you can get a much higher price than your creditor.

- **Creditor Sale.** The final way that a creditor can dispose of your car is by selling the car at a public or private sale. During the sale of your car, the creditor must follow certain rules. If the creditor does not, you can sue the creditor to stop the sale and to recover money damages. Two of the most important rules are: (1) the creditor must give you notice of the sale, and (2) the sale must be "commercially reasonable." Both of these rules will be discussed in detail below.

Did the Consumer Get Notice of the Creditor's Sale?

Notice of sale is very important as it tells you when you will no longer be able to redeem your car. If you do not act before the date of sale, you will lose the car. Notice of sale may be the first time that you hear from your creditor after repossession if you waived your right to notice of acceleration or if your state does not have a "right to cure" law.

The creditor must give "reasonable notification," which means he must give the debtor sufficient time to take appropriate steps to protect his interests. The timing of notice differs in each state, but creditors usually give you notice of sale ten days beforehand. The notice must be written and accurate in every respect, and most courts require that it specify whether it will be a public or private sale and the time and place of a public sale, or the time after which a private sale will be made.

Some courts have barred the creditor from collecting a deficiency judgment where the creditor failed to send the debtor notice even though the debtor actually knew about the sale from another source. Courts have also forced the creditor to pay the debtor the amount that the sale price is diminished because of inadequate notice.

Was the Creditor's Sale Commercially Reasonable?

The creditor sale must be "commercially reasonable" in every way. Commercial reasonableness is not defined, but it is more than creditor convenience. Commercial reasonableness includes the following:

- **Creditor use of car.** A creditor's use of the car before sale could be commercially unreasonable. When the car is in the creditor's custody, the creditor has a duty to use reasonable care. If the car is destroyed while in the creditor's possession, the creditor may no longer be entitled to any deficiency. In general, the creditor cannot drive the debtor's car unless it is to preserve the car's value—never for personal reasons.

- **Creditor reconditioning the car.** It may be commercially unreasonable for a creditor to sell the car in its "then condition" if preparing the car in some minimal way could significantly increase its value. The creditor may have to "recondition" the car including polishing, cleaning, tune-ups and paint touch-ups. At the same time, you should make sure the creditor does not put too much work into reconditioning the car, because you will end up paying for all reasonable expenses of car preparation for sale. The amount of reconditioning should be proportionate to the value of the car or must result in a significant increase in the sale price.

- **Creditor delay of sale.** The creditor cannot unreasonably delay the sale of the car. If the creditor holds onto a car for too long, the creditor may be barred from collecting any deficiency, and may have to accept the car for the rest of the amount due on the loan. (See "strict foreclosure" under Creditor Disposition). On the other hand, a sale that is too hasty could be commercially unreasonable if it results in inadequate advertising or in a failure to produce a sufficient number of bidders. If the debtor already paid 60% or more of the loan, the sale must be within 90 days. To determine whether a delay is commercially reasonable, check how much the car has depreciated during the delay, and consider the storage costs and other seasonal and regional considerations.

- **Creditor choice between public and private sale.** The choice between a public and private sale must be commercially reasonable and must maximize sale proceeds. However, a low sale price by itself is probably not enough to prove that a sale was commercially unreasonable. You should check wholesale pricing guides, like the publication put out by the National Automobile Dealers Association, to determine whether a sale price was commercially reasonable.

The creditor must make the car available for inspection before a public auction. If you see that a creditor's preparation for sale is clearly inadequate or if the creditor appears to be selling to itself at a low price, you can try to stop the sale. At a public sale, you can bid for your car. You can also offer to purchase your car at a private sale.

Is There Any Deficiency After Creditor Sale?

After sale of the car, the sale proceeds would first be applied to the reasonable expenses of repossession, then to reasonable expenses of the sale, then to satisfaction of the debt. Whatever is left over (the surplus) must go to the debtor. If there is not enough to cover all these expenses and the remaining debt, the debtor may owe the creditor the amount of the loan and expenses that exceed the sale price, called the deficiency. Under state laws, however, the creditor's right to a deficiency may be restricted. Some state laws preclude the creditor from getting a deficiency, or may limit the deficiency amount if the creditor elected "strict foreclosure," if there was a commercially unreasonable disposition of the car, or if the creditor did not comply with specific notice requirements under state law.

If you owe a deficiency, you should recalculate the deficiency amount to make sure it is correct. Make sure the following is accurate:

- **The remainder due on the loan before adjustments.** Obtain the original credit documents, recalculate the total amount due and make sure the credit rates are not higher than your state limits.

- **Unearned interest rebates.** The total payment of a pre-computed loan includes interest payments over the full loan term. When a creditor accelerates the loan payments, the creditor is seeking payment earlier than scheduled so the amount of interest that you owe decrcases. The creditor should rebate this unearned interest to you, and the rebate should be computed based on a formula specified in the loan agreement or based on state law, whichever is more favorable to the debtor, as of the date of acceleration.

- **Interest and penalties after acceleration.** After rebating the unearned interest, your state's laws or the credit agreement may authorize the creditor to charge interest on the amount due from the date of acceleration until you repay this amount. It depends on state law and the contract, but usually late payment charges will not be permitted after the time of acceleration or at the time a deficiency judgment is rendered. A creditor cannot charge both late-payment and extra-interest charges for the same period.

- **Prepaid insurance premiums.** You should cancel any prepaid insurance and get a rebate. Also, you should make sure that the creditor does not charge for reconditioning and repairing a car if it is covered by the car's service contract or extended warranty.

- **Value of car.** Make sure you are credited the sale price of the car at retail, not the estimated value.

- **Expenses from repossession and sale.** All expenses must be reasonable, including all repossession, storage, repair, reconditioning, and advertising expenses. The creditor cannot charge you more than the amount the creditor was actually charged. Expenses for sale should be the same as for the creditor's non-repossessed cars. Any attorneys' fees and legal expenses must be reasonable and are governed by the credit agreement and by state law.

CHAPTER 18

How to Buy a House With Marks on Your Credit

If you have any negative marks on your credit—such as a late payment, default, repossession, lien, judgment or bankruptcy—you probably think you'll never be able to buy a house. Not so. If you have a steady and secure income that is high enough so you can afford to make the monthly payments, and you have a sufficient sum of money saved for a down payment, you will probably be able to buy a house.

Think of it this way. For most lenders, making a home loan is a very safe investment. For the one thing, the loan will be secured by the house. If you don't make the payments, the lender can foreclose. In addition, in today's economy, all across the country house values are rising or remaining steady—that is, they are not going down. The $125,000 house you buy today may be worth $135,000 a year from now, simply by virtue of the economy. Even if you do default and the lender must foreclose, the lender will make back its investment, and possibly more.

Before You Start Looking

Nothing will frustrate you more than finding your dream house and then being denied a loan. Before you go house or loan shopping, do a little preparation.

Estimate how much house you can afford.

As a general rule, most people can afford a house worth about two and a half times their gross annual income, assuming a moderate amount of other long-term debts. If you have no other long-term debts, you may be able to afford something three or four times your annual income.

Gather your paperwork.

Make sure you have a copy of:

- a recent pay stub;
- last year's tax return;
- names and account numbers for your car lender, student loan holder, credit card issuers and other creditors;
- checking, savings and money market account numbers, balances and bank names;
- a list of your assets (other real estate, retirement plans, vehicles, etc.); and
- a copy of your credit report.

Be sure you know what's in your credit report, as anyone to whom you apply for financing will pull a copy.

Get a loan prequalification letter.

This is a letter stating that you have been "prequalified" for a loan up to a certain amount, based on your income and credit history, and how much you'll need for a down payment and closing costs. It stops short of guaranteeing ultimate loan approval, but it makes it clear that loan approval is all but certain. Any house purchase offer that comes with a prequalification letter will be that much more attractive to a seller who might be worried about the buyer's ability to get a loan. For someone with compromised credit, a prequalification letter is often a must. A letter will state that you have been approved for a loan of up to "X" amount of money at an interest rate of "Y" or less.

To get such a letter, make an appointment with (or call) several lenders or mortgage brokers, discuss your financial situation and find out if you can prequalify. You are not shopping for the best loan with the most competitive rates; you simply want to make sure you can qualify for a loan. If you don't have the time or inclination to call around, consider working with a loan broker, a person who specializes in matching house buyers with mortgage lenders. Loan brokers subscribe to different computer systems that list various mortgages available in an area. Most often, a loan broker is paid by the lender, so it won't cost you money to use one. Because loan brokers have access to so many different lending sources, they can usually find a lender to help you.

Conventional Loans

As you learn about available loans, you may be overwhelmed by the range of terms. Down payment requirements, interest rates, loan application fees and points (a fee charged by a lender for the privilege of making you a loan, expressed as a percentage of the loan amount) can vary tremendously among lenders and even with the same lender. One reason is simple competition. But another reason is that different types of loans are made available to different types of borrowers. What separates one borrower from the next is often each person's credit history.

A loans

For many years, mortgage lenders wrote only A loans. An A loan was available to a person with flawless credit—someone who had paid every personal loan, student loan, credit card bill and existing mortgage payment on time. Occasionally, a person with a minor credit blip, such as a one-time late payment on an otherwise perfectly paid loan, would still qualify for an A loan. A loans typically require little money down and charge the most favorable interest rate. Anyone who didn't qualify for an A loan had only two choices: forego buying a home until all the negative marks came off the credit report, or borrow from a lender who required a huge down payment and charged near-credit-card interest rates.

Many mortgage lenders now write B and C loans for people with somewhat marred credit histories and D loans for people with very bad credit histories. The following describes B, C and D loans.

B loans

Some lenders require clean credit for the previous 12 months, but allow a few missed payments before that. Others permit one or two late mortgage payments, one late personal or student loan payment and few late credit card payments during the previous year. Late payments cannot be more than 60 days past due. B loans usually require more money down; interest rates are usually one or two percentage points higher than A loans.

C loans

Some lenders require clean credit for the previous 12 months, but allow a serious credit problem, such as a bankruptcy or foreclosure, a few years before. Others permit three or four late mortgage payments, five or six late loan or credit card payments or late payments more than 60 days past due. C loans usually require even more money down; interest rates are usually one to four percentage points higher than A loans.

D loans

D loans are available to people with very bad credit histories—bankruptcy or foreclosure in the past year, or habitual late payments on loans and bills. D loans usually require lots of money down; interest rates can be 100% higher than what they are for A loans.

Improving Your Qualification

If you don't currently qualify for a conventional loan, consider doing any of the following to improve your chances.

- **Wait a while.** In the mean time, you can save more money to make a larger down payment, watch some of the older negatives on your credit report drop off and get more positive recent information into your credit report.

- **Move to a more affordable area.** If what's holding you back from qualifying for a loan is that you have too little money saved for the down payment, move to an area where your savings will go further.

- **Buy with someone with whom you'll live.** You can improve your chances of qualifying for a loan if you'll apply with someone with excellent credit. We are not suggesting that you marry (or move in with) the first available person to come your way. But perhaps you have a friend who is house hunting, too. You can buy a two-unit building and apply for one mortgage for the entire purchase.

- **Have the seller help you.** The more money the seller kicks in towards closing costs, the less you have to pay towards them. This can free up additional funds to be used towards a larger down payment and possibly make you a better credit risk which in turn may help you qualify for a lower interest rate.

Other Ways to Finance a House Purchase

Obtaining a conventional loan from a mortgage lender is not the only way to finance the purchase of your house.

Private financing

Consider approaching a financially well-off friend or relative for a loan. Propose a written business deal. Ask to borrow the money at a rate less than you'd pay a conventional lender but more than your friend would earn on his money invested conservatively. For example, if the bank would charge you 7.25% for a mortgage loan, but would pay your friend Allan only 5% on his mutual fund, ask Allan to lend you the money at 6.5%—a deal for you both.

Seller financing

Some sellers don't need or want the money from the sale quite yet. Perhaps the seller will owe taxes on the profit or be concerned about losing the money to a long-term health facility. No matter what the reason, suggest to the seller that she "carry the note." This means that you pay her your down payment and monthly mortgage payments; a mortgage lender is not involved. While the seller should do a credit check and request a copy of your pay stub, her qualifying standards will be far less rigorous than a conventional lender's.

Mortgage buydown

These are generally available to people buying a new home in a new housing development. The developer prepays part of your mortgage payment for a few years to help you qualify for a loan. Some conventional lenders have provided buydowns for people buying existing, not new, homes. These loans can get you into hot water, so be careful. When you move into a new home, you will have lots of expenses. If you take on long term debt during the first few years you are in your home, the increasing mortgage payments may become unaffordable.

Public financing

Many state, county or local governments provide mortgage financing to first time homebuyers willing to buy in a "target" area, typically a low-income area, some of which have serious social problems. If this is an option you would consider, you may be in luck. These programs are generally available to people with moderate income who can afford a low down payment and closing costs, and can afford the monthly payments. Credit requirements are often relaxed somewhat.

The Lesson

Don't despair. As one mortgage broker once said, "Find me someone with bad credit and I'll find her a loan. Mortgage loans are safe and secure to a lender, who makes money by making loans, not by turning people down."

CHAPTER 19

What to Do When You Can't Pay the Mortgage

If you're having trouble making your house payments, the first thing you should know is that you are not alone. Home mortgage defaults have been at an all-time high across America. This is good news for you, because it means that mortgage lenders are familiar with people in default on their home loans and often have established programs and policies to deal with such situations.

Let's begin with a definition.

"Foreclosure" is the right of a mortgage lender to sell your house at a public auction and keep the proceeds if you fall behind on your mortgage and don't take steps to get back on track or work out another solution. There are two different kinds of foreclosure. One is called a "judicial foreclosure" because the lender must file papers in court and obtain the court's approval before foreclosing. This kind of foreclosure can take as long as 18-36 months before you would ever lose your house. Most states have judicial foreclosures. If you signed only a traditional mortgage note when you purchased or refinanced your property, your lender probably must use a judicial foreclosure to sell your house.

The other kind of foreclosure is called a "non-judicial foreclosure" because the lender does not have to go to court in order to foreclose. Instead, a third-party trustee sells your property after sending you a series of notices. The trustee is the person or business named in a deed of trust which you signed instead of, or in addition to, a traditional mortgage when you purchased or refinanced your property. Non-judicial foreclosures can happen quickly, sometimes in as few as four months.

It's very important that you know if you signed only a traditional mortgage or a deed of trust. Your options for dealing with your house may depend on how much time you have.

You also need to determine your ultimate goal. Is it to save your house at all costs? Let it go for the minimum possible damage to your credit? The options you want to pursue will depend on your desired outcome.

So what are those options?

Find Money to Get or Stay Current

As odd as it sounds, some people never consider borrowing money from friends or relatives to get current on their home loan. This is probably not an option for someone substantially behind on payments, someone unemployed or otherwise unable to catch up, or someone who wants to unload the property. But if you need help for a month or two, consider asking those who love you most and would want to help you out.

In addition, if someone co-signed your loan for you when you bought or refinanced, go to that person at once. First, you have an ethical duty to let the person know you are at risk of defaulting or that you already have. Secondly, your co-signer will want to avoid damaging his or her credit file and may lend you the money to get and stay current, share in the monthly payments or take over payments until you work out another solution.

Contact Your Lender

Maybe this is obvious. But if you want to keep your house and you are having trouble paying your mortgage—even if your lender has started the foreclosure process—contact the lender and try to work out a deal.

Before taking back your house, your lender would rather rewrite your loan, suspend principal payments for a while (have you pay interest only), reduce your payments, let you miss a few payments and spread them out over time or give you an interest-free loan to get current. Why would a lender do any of these things? Mortgage lenders are in the business of making money. They don't make money by trying to resell distressed (a term used to describe a piece of property that's been foreclosed on) real estate. They do make money when you make payments, particularly interest payments, on an outstanding loan.

If your loan is held by the federal government (Fannie Mae or Freddie Mac), you may have some extra good news. In 1997, both programs made radical changes to their home loan default programs, emphasizing foreclosure prevention whenever possible. Both Fannie Mae and Freddie Mac offer rate reductions, term extensions and other loan modifications for people experiencing involuntary money problems. One option would allow you to make reduced payments for up to 18 months. If you can't get help from your loan servicer, you can call either loan holder directly at 202-752-7000 (Fannie Mae) or 800-373-3343 (Freddie Mac).

Keep in mind one thing: If you truly can't afford to keep your house, negotiating for a new loan or temporary suspension of payments may not help you in the long run. You may be wasting your time and money if you try desperately to hold onto a house you honestly can't afford.

Find a Good Mortgage Broker

Again, this is an option to consider if you want to hold onto your house. If you have tried negotiating with the lender and can't come up with a deal that you can afford, don't give up. A mortgage broker, a person who works independent of any particular lender to find you the best possible home loan, might know of more options. Good mortgage brokers have access to information about hundreds of loans offered by banks, savings and loans, finance companies and other mortgage lenders. You may find yourself able to refinance to at least temporarily bring your payments down dramatically.

Consider the case of Tony, who several years ago had a fixed rate mortgage at 11%. After he lost his job, he struggled for months to make his house payments. Then he met with a mortgage broker who knew about an adjustable rate mortgage that started at 3%, rising 1% every six months. Tony jumped at the loan, brought his payments down significantly, and was able to keep his house while he spent an another full year looking for a new job. After the interest rate climbed above the going rate for mortgages, Tony refinanced again, and currently has a loan at 7.5%.

Contact Your Private Mortgage Insurer

If you made a down payment on your house of less than 20% of the purchase price, your lender probably required you to take out something called private mortgage insurance, or PMI. You were required to buy PMI because by borrowing more than 80% of the purchase price, you are in greater risk of default than is someone who borrows 80% or less. When you took out the loan, you probably cursed the extra amount you were required to pay each month for PMI. But if you're having trouble paying your loan, PMI could actually help you. The insurance company may lend you money to meet any shortage to prevent foreclosure.

Sell the Property

You are certainly better off selling the house than having it go to foreclosure. If you can find a buyer who will offer to pay at least what you owe your lender, take the offer. Ideally, you will find a buyer who is willing to pay the amount you owe your lender and any other lienholders, such as a second mortgage lender or the IRS if the taxing agency has recorded a lien against you for unpaid taxes. There are investors who specialize in buying real estate heading for foreclosure. You won't get top dollar and you may lose any equity you have in the property, but still it's better than having the lender foreclose or giving the house back to the lender to avoid foreclosure.

When listing your house with a real estate agent, make sure that you are being realistic about the sales price. Often, real estate agents will tell you they can get a high price for your home, because that is what you want to hear. However, if what you really need is a quick sale you might want to think of listing your home for less than the going rate. What you need is for the home to sell for an amount more than the mortgage balance before the auction date. Sellers in foreclosure often get greedy and try to get the highest price possible only to watch their house sit on the market without any takers and get foreclosed.

Be careful of people who advertise as pre-foreclosure investors, however. Some of them are sharks. For example, don't agree to deed your house to someone who promises to sell it for you. The person will more likely collect rent from you, not make any mortgage payments, not try to sell the property and just let the lender foreclose. Although the deed isn't in your name, the mortgage still is and you are still liable on it. The foreclosure will go on your credit record and you may owe any shortfall between the auction price and your total balance due.

In addition, be sure to get all understandings in writing. If you have any doubts about the person with whom you are dealing, ask for the names and phone numbers of references, and call them. Then call your local Better Business Bureau and your state Department of Real Estate to ask about the investor. If anything sounds fishy, don't pursue the deal.

You may be anxious to walk away from your house because it has depreciated in value and you owe your lender more than the house is worth. Up until a few years ago, you would have had a hard time selling your house under such circumstances. That's because your lender can block any sale if it won't bring in at least the amount that you owe the lender.

But lenders began to realize that getting something is better than getting nothing. Today, many lenders will agree to a "short sale." This is a situation in which the sale of the house brings in less than you owe the lender, but the lender agrees to forgive a portion or all of the difference.

A lender will not agree to a short sale unless, in advance of the sale, you provide documentation of financial or medical hardship you are experiencing—that is, unless you can justify to the lender why you are having trouble paying. Divorce, job layoff, illness or death can be acceptable reasons. So is a lack of cash reserves because of extraordinary and unexpected expenses, such as a required move due to a job change resulting in your paying the mortgage on your old house and housing expenses for your new home.

As mentioned, documentation is key. Be prepared to provide your lender with recent tax returns (anywhere from one to three years) and one of the following types of information:

- letters from doctors documenting health problems
- efforts of your job search
- divorce decree specifying who pays what and default notices if your spouse was ordered to pay bills but has not
- efforts you've made to sell your home

Deed the Property Back to the Lender

If you get no offers for your house or the lender won't approve a short sale—which especially may be the case if your loan is held by Fannie Mae or Freddie Mac or was issued by the Federal Housing Administration—consider walking away from your house. Call the lender and ask if it will accept your deed in lieu of foreclosing. Many will. Be aware that this can be a huge negative mark on your credit report. Don't do this hastily.

If the lender won't, prepare what's called a quitclaim deed—you "quit" your interest in the property and transfer ownership to your lender. You write DEED IN LIEU OF FORECLOSURE in block capital letters across the top of the deed, pay any transfer fee, record the quitclaim deed where you recorded your ownership deed and mail a copy of the recorded quitclaim deed to the lender. You no longer own the house. Your lender does. However, the lender may refuse to accept the property and transfer it back to you.

Tax Ramifications of a Short Sale or Deed in Lieu of Foreclosure

If your lender forgives at least $600 from a short sale or after auctioning off a house you deed back, the lender will be required to issue an IRS Form 1099 report of miscellaneous income at the end of the tax year. When you file your tax return, you must include on your tax return the amount of income shown on the 1099.

You won't owe taxes on the money if you wipe out the debt in bankruptcy before filing your tax return or you were insolvent at the time the creditor forgave the debt. The Tax Code does not define insolvent. Generally, it means that your debts exceed the value of your assets at the time the debt was forgiven. To figure out whether or not you are insolvent, you will have to total up your assets and your debts, including the debt that was forgiven.

For more information, see chapter 6, "Beware of the IRS If You Settle or Default on a Debt."

Declare Bankruptcy

Bankruptcy will stop a foreclosure in its tracks. This is because a bankruptcy filing puts into place something called the "automatic stay," which stops virtually all of your creditors from attempting to collect your debts.

There are two types of consumer bankruptcies—Chapter 7 and Chapter 13. Chapter 7 is essentially a liquidation case, where your nonessential property may be sold to pay off your creditors. If you're behind on your mortgage and you file for Chapter 7 bankruptcy, the foreclosure may be stopped only temporarily. You cannot make up back payments in Chapter 7 or try to get back on track with your mortgage. Instead, the lender will probably ask that the automatic stay be lifted so that it can proceed with the foreclosure. The bankruptcy court will probably grant the request.

The other kind of bankruptcy, Chapter 13, is a reorganization bankruptcy. You must have disposable income to fund a repayment plan. In a Chapter 13 case, you can make up your mortgage arrears as a part of your plan as long as you immediately begin to make the regular payments called for in your contract. However, you will need to make at least the regular payment while in bankruptcy. If you can't make at least the regular payment now, a Chapter 13 bankruptcy may not be able to help you keep your home.

Chapter 7 and 13 bankruptcies have a number of eligibility requirements. See Chapter 20, "Is Bankruptcy Right for Me."

CHAPTER 20

Bankruptcy: Is It Right for Me?

Most people think of bankruptcy as a process in which you go to court and get your debts erased. But in fact, there are two types of bankruptcies: the familiar liquidation bankruptcy, where your debts are wiped out (Chapter 7 bankruptcy) and reorganization bankruptcy, where you partially or fully repay your debts. The reorganization bankruptcy for individuals is called Chapter 13 bankruptcy. (There are two other kinds of reorganization bankruptcy: Chapter 11, for businesses and for individuals with debts over $1 million, and Chapter 12, for family farmers.)

Filing for bankruptcy puts into effect something called the "automatic stay," which immediately stops your creditors from trying to collect. Creditors cannot garnish your wages, empty your bank account or go after your car or house.

Until your bankruptcy case ends, your financial problems are in the hands of the bankruptcy court. The court exercises its control through a court-appointed person called a "bankruptcy trustee." The trustee's primary duty is to see that your creditors are paid as much as possible.

Chapter 7 Bankruptcy—An Overview

Chapter 7 bankruptcy is sometimes called "straight" bankruptcy. It cancels all or most of your debts; in exchange, you might have to surrender some property. It takes up to six months and costs approximately $175 in filing fees.

To file for Chapter 7 bankruptcy, you fill out several forms describing your property, income, monthly living expenses, debts, exempt property—the property you keep through bankruptcy, any property you sold or gave away and money you spent during the previous two years. The trustee reviews your papers at a short hearing, called the "creditors' meeting," which you must attend. Creditors may attend, too, but rarely do. After this meeting, the trustee collects your nonexempt property to sell to pay your creditors. If the property isn't worth very much or would be cumbersome to sell, the trustee can abandon the property, meaning you get to keep it.

Chapter 7 Bankruptcy— When It Might Not Help

Filing for Chapter 7 bankruptcy is only one way to solve debt problems. In several situations, Chapter 7 bankruptcy may not be the right choice.

You previously received a bankruptcy discharge. You cannot file for Chapter 7 bankruptcy if you obtained a discharge of your debts under Chapter 7 or Chapter 13 in a case begun within the past six years.

A previous bankruptcy case was dismissed. You cannot file for Chapter 7 bankruptcy if a previous Chapter 7 or Chapter 13 case was dismissed within the past 180 days because you violated a court order or requested the dismissal after a creditor asked for relief from the automatic stay.

A friend or relative co-signed a loan. Anyone who co-signed a loan or otherwise took on a joint obligation with you can be held wholly responsible for the debt if you file for Chapter 7 bankruptcy.

You could pay your debts over three to five years. A bankruptcy judge who decides you have enough assets or income to repay your debts can dismiss your Chapter 7 bankruptcy case or convert it to a Chapter 13 bankruptcy.

You defrauded your creditors. Bankruptcy is geared toward the honest debtor who got in too deep and needs the help of the bankruptcy court to get a fresh start. If you have engaged in any questionable activities, such as unloading assets to your friends or relatives to hide them from creditors, incurring debts for non-necessities when you were clearly broke, or lying about your income or debts on a credit application, your case may be thrown out.

You recently incurred debts for luxuries. If you've recently run up large debts for a vacation, hobby or entertainment, filing for bankruptcy probably won't help you. Most luxury debts incurred just before filing are not dischargeable if the creditor objects.

You expect debts for necessities. If you expect to incur more debts for necessities, such as additional medical costs you anticipate because of an existing illness, consider delaying filing for bankruptcy. Debts you incur after you file will not be discharged.

Chapter 7 Bankruptcy— Will It Discharge Enough of Your Debts?

Certain debts cannot be discharged in Chapter 7 bankruptcy. These are called nondischargeable debts, and it doesn't make sense to file for Chapter 7 if your primary goal is to get rid of them. In general, they are:

- back child support and alimony
- student loans that first became due fewer than seven years ago
- court-ordered restitution
- income taxes less than three years past due, and
- court judgments for injuries or death to someone arising from your intoxicated driving.

Furthermore, the bankruptcy judge can rule any of the following debts nondischargeable if the creditor objects in the bankruptcy court:

- debts incurred on the basis of fraud, such as lying on a credit application
- debts from willful or malicious injury to another or another's property
- debts from larceny (theft), breach of trust or embezzlement, and
- debts you are obligated to pay under a divorce settlement.

Chapter 7 Bankruptcy— How Much Property Will You Have to Give Up?

Whether or not you file for Chapter 7 bankruptcy may depend on what property will be taken to pay your creditors-your nonexempt property. In most states, you can keep the following items (this list varies greatly from state to state):

- a motor vehicle, to a certain value
- reasonably needed clothing
- reasonably needed household furnishings, goods and appliances

- jewelry, to a certain value, and personal effects
- life insurance (cash or loan value, or proceeds), to a certain value
- pensions and retirement plans
- part of the equity in your home
- tools of your trade or profession, to a certain value
- portion of unpaid but earned wages, and
- public benefits (welfare, Social Security, unemployment compensation) accumulated in a bank account.

If you've pledged property as collateral for a loan, the loan is called secured. The most common examples are house and motor vehicle loans. In most cases, you'll either have to surrender the collateral to the creditor or make arrangements to pay for it during or after bankruptcy.

Maybe Chapter 13 Bankruptcy Is a Better Choice

Chapter 13 bankruptcy is different from Chapter 7. Instead of asking the court to wipe out your debts, you propose a three to five year repayment plan under which you pay all or a portion of your debts. To file for Chapter 13 bankruptcy, you fill out the same forms as you would for a Chapter 7 case, plus your proposed repayment plan. If the court accepts your plan, you make payments to the bankruptcy trustee who distributes a share to your creditors.

There are many reasons why people choose Chapter 13 bankruptcy, and in particular, Chapter 13 over Chapter 7. Generally, you are probably a good candidate for Chapter 13 bankruptcy if you are in any of the following situations:

- You are behind on your mortgage or car loan and want to make up the missed payments and reinstate the original agreement. You cannot do this in Chapter 7 bankruptcy. You can in Chapter 13 bankruptcy.
- You owe federal income taxes. Unless you meet several conditions, you cannot discharge federal income taxes in Chapter 7 bankruptcy. You can use Chapter 13 bankruptcy to pay the IRS over time.
- You have property you'd lose if you filed Chapter 7 bankruptcy.
- You received a Chapter 7 discharge within the previous six years.
- You have a co-debtor on a personal debt.

- You have a sincere desire to repay your debts, but you need the protection of the bankruptcy court to do so.

Chapter 13 Bankruptcy—Are You Eligible?

Chapter 13 bankruptcy has a number of eligibility requirements.

Your debts must not be too high. You will not qualify for Chapter 13 bankruptcy if your secured debts exceed $750,000. A debt is secured if you stand to lose specific property if you don't make your payments to the creditor. Home loans and car loans are common examples of secured debts. But a debt might also be secured if a creditor—such as the IRS—has filed a lien on your property.

In addition, your unsecured debts cannot exceed $250,000. An unsecured debt is any debt for which you haven't pledged collateral. Most debts are unsecured, including credit cards, medical bills, student loans and department store charges.

You must have stable and regular income. This doesn't mean you must earn the same amount every month. But the income must be steady-likely to continue, and periodic-weekly, monthly, quarterly, semi-annual or seasonal.

You must have disposable income. Your income must be high enough so that after you pay for your basic needs, you will have money left over to make periodic payments to the trustee. To determine if your disposable income is high enough, you must create a monthly budget. If the trustee or a creditor thinks your budget includes expenses other than necessities, it may be challenged.

You May Be Able to Avoid Bankruptcy Altogether

Although bankruptcy is sometimes promoted as an "easy" solution to financial problems, it can be quite painful and carries consequences for years to come. Your bankruptcy will be listed on your credit report for up to ten years, even if you file but don't go through with it, and can make it difficult or expensive to get credit, jobs or insurance. There are often many negative lasting emotions that some people experience as a result of filing bankruptcy.

As an alternative to bankruptcy, Debt Counselors of America® offers a program, called One-Pay®, to help consumers who are having financial problems. Through the program, consumers are able to repay their debts without having to file bankruptcy.

CHAPTER 21

What to Do to Never File Bankruptcy Again

There are no magic rules that will solve everyone's financial troubles. But several suggestions should help you stay out of financial hot water. If you have a family, everyone will have to participate. No one person can do all the work alone. So make sure your spouse or partner, and the kids, understand that the family is having financial difficulties and agree together to take the steps that will lead to recovery.

Create a Realistic Spending Plan and Stick to It

For several months, make lists of every outlay of cash or cash equivalent used to make purchases. Also track all of your income for those months. When you are done tracking your expenses, make a list of each category of expenses, and write down the total amount you spent in that category per month (taking an average if you tracked expenses for two months). At the bottom of the list, write down your average monthly income.

With these figures, you can make a spending plan. Your list of expenses indicates how much you project spending each month. If the total exceeds your income or leaves you with little left over, you will have to cut back.

For an easy web-based way to create a spending plan, visit the On-Track[sm] program offered by Debt Counselors of America® at www.GetOutOfDebt.org.

Once you have your spending plan, don't let it sit in your desk collecting dust or remain on the computer never to be revisited. You need to compare your actual expenses to your projected expenses in order to keep yourself heading in the right direction. One way to do this is to create 12 columns (corresponding to the months of the year) next to your projected expenses on your spending plan. Each day, record the amount of money you spend in the various categories for the current month. Keep a running subtotal so you know when you are approaching your total projected expenses for the month. Be sure not to exceed it and to leave yourself enough money to pay all necessary monthly expenses.

A spending plan gives you the flexibility to spend more than you anticipated in any given category or categories. Knowing the monthly "pot" of money you have to spend means that when you go over in one area, you simply cut back in others.

Shop Smart

Many people get into financial hot water because they fail to plan their shopping. Here are a few ideas to help you avoid this trap.

- Don't grocery shop on an empty stomach. Most people spend as much as 50% more than they normally would when they grocery shop while they are hungry. Extra items purchased tend to be snack items and "junk food" associated with curing hunger pangs quickly. By shopping after you have eaten, you are more likely to buy only what you need.
- Don't impulse buy. When you see something you hadn't planned to buy, don't purchase it on the spot. Go home and think it over. It's unlikely you'll return to the store and buy it. This holds true just as much for a $15 book as it does for a $1,500 computer.
- Don't buy at a sale simply for the sake of it being a sale. Buying a $500 item on sale for $400 isn't a $100 savings if you didn't need the item to begin with. It's spending $400 unnecessarily.

Cut Your Expenses

Cutting your expenses is similar to shopping smart. Here are a few suggestions.

- Shrink food costs by buying what you need on sale, purchasing generic brands, buying in bulk and shopping at discount outlets.
- Improve your gas mileage by tuning your car, checking the air in the tires and driving less—carpool, work at home, ride your bicycle, walk, take the bus or train and combine trips.
- Discontinue cable, or at least the premium channels, and subscriptions to magazines and newspapers.

- Use your local library to borrow books, CDs and videos and to read magazines and newspapers.

- Make long-distance calls only when necessary and at off-peak hours. Compare long distance carriers to make sure you are getting the best deal. If all long-distance carriers will charge you about the same, take advantage of checks (often around $50) sent to urge you to switch carriers.

Get Medical Insurance If Possible

Many people who file for bankruptcy had no health insurance or were significantly under insured. You can't avoid medical emergencies, but you may be able to avoid financial ruin. Call around. Many companies offer both group and individual policies. Even a stopgap policy with a large deductible can help if a medical crisis comes up. Federal law prohibits you from being denied medical insurance because of a pre-existing condition. Furthermore, if you anticipate leaving a job shortly, federal law requires that you be offered medical insurance through your former employer for up to 18 months after you leave. (Of course, you must pay for the total cost of the coverage plus a small administrative fee.) If you have trouble finding coverage on your own, contact a medical insurance broker to shop around for you.

Don't Carry Credit Card Balances

For many people, dependence on credit cards is what got them into financial trouble. Credit cards can feel like a painless way to spend, while nothing may be further from the truth. The average American owes several thousands of dollars on her credit cards. While only 5% of people are behind in their payments, a full 60% carry a balance each month, incurring finance charges somewhere around 18% a year. You don't have to live like that. Consider tossing all of your credit cards in a drawer (or in the garbage) and to commit to living without credit. If you insist on using credit, only charge what you can currently pay for and pay off your balance in full when the bill arrives. Don't charge based on future income; sometimes future income doesn't materialize or it materializes but you need the money to pay for an emergency expense.

If you're ready to live without credit, it's time to close those unnecessary accounts. Just cutting up your card and tossing it in the trash does not close your credit card account. The safest way to close a credit card account is by sending a certified letter, return receipt requested to the customer service department of the card issuer. Ask the card issuer to close your account and to report your account to credit bureaus as "closed by consumer." You can close your account even if you haven't paid off the balance-the card issuer will close your account but still send you your monthly statements until you pay it off in full. In approximately ten days, the card issuer should send you a letter confirming that your account is "closed by the consumer." If you don't receive the confirmation letter, follow up by calling the card issuer to make sure it closed your card and is reporting it properly to the credit bureaus. You may even want to get another copy of your credit report to make sure it is reported correctly. To receive a consolidated credit report, visit www.GetOutOfDebt.org.

Avoid Large Rent or House Payments

Most people have a choice in how much to spend for housing. If you are a renter and your rent is unmanageable, explore other options. Consider moving to a different neighborhood or into smaller digs, or taking in a roommate. If you live in a "renter's market," where high vacancy rates mean that landlords are desperate for new tenants or to hang onto the ones they have, ask for a rent reduction. If you're a long-time tenant with a good relationship with your landlord, he may be willing to lower your rent so that you stay and he can avoid the hassle of looking for someone new.

If you are a homeowner or you are in the market to buy, be realistic about how much you can afford. Lenders have all kinds of mortgages available both to buyers and to owners looking to refinance. Many mortgages start out low and gradually increase over time, hopefully to correspond to an increase in your income. Don't take on something you can't handle. For example, a lender might offer you a bi-weekly mortgage, where you make a payment every other week, not once a month. The attraction is that you will pay off your mortgage faster than you would with a standard mortgage and save interest. But you are obligating yourself to make 26 payments a year, which equals 13 months of payments, not 12. A better alternative is to take out a standard once a month mortgage and add some extra money when you have it, rather than obligate yourself to make extra payments you might not have.

Similarly, if you are going through a divorce, think carefully before agreeing to keep the house. Money problems and divorce are intertwined for many couples. You will have that much more difficult a time making the payments as a single person than you did while married. The house may have sentimental value for you, but very few people hold onto their homes for more than seven years.

Don't Co-sign or Guarantee a Loan for Someone

Your signature obligates you as if you were the primary borrower. You can never be sure that the other person will pay. The lender is not required to try and collect from the primary borrower before coming after you. If you wind up paying the debt, you could go after the primary borrower for repayment, but good luck. If she didn't have the money to pay the lender, she probably won't have it to pay you. And if she files for bankruptcy, you will be solely liable for the debt.

Don't Join Finances with Someone Who Has Questionable Spending Habits

If you incur a joint debt, you are liable for all of it if the other person defaults. If you combine your incomes into one bank account, the other person can empty the account, leaving nothing there when the bills come due. This rule even applies for a spouse. Although most spouses don't keep their financial lives separate, it is worthwhile to do so if you can avoid financial disaster.

Don't Put *All* of Your Money Into High-Risk Investments

Invest some of your money conservatively, opting for some certificates of deposit, money market funds and government bonds. Limit riskier investments such as speculative real estate, penny stocks and junk bonds.

CHAPTER 22

Making a Clean Financial Break at Divorce

If you're going through a divorce, you're probably exhausted by the emotional upheaval and the day-to-day details of carving out a new, separate life.

One thing that's easily overlooked—or outright ignored—in the turmoil of divorce is what your financial picture will look like down the road. Some people just want out of their marriage as quickly as possible and don't consider the financial ramifications of their actions. But you need to slow down some and look to the future. No doubt, your financial life has been intertwined with your spouse's during your marriage. Perhaps financial struggles even contributed to the end of your marriage; that's not unusual. While it's not always possible to sever the financial cord with your soon-to-be-ex-spouse 100% (if you have minor children, either you will be ordered to pay child support or you will be entitled to receive it), if it is at all possible to make a clean break when dividing the property and allocating the debts, do so. If you stay connected to your ex-spouse financially, you're at risk.

Dividing Property

At divorce, some basic rules apply in dividing marital property. First of all, you are entitled to divide your property any way you want. It really doesn't matter what the laws of your state say. They apply only if you and your spouse can't agree on the division of property and take your dispute to court for a judge to decide. Otherwise, you're free to divide your property in the way that makes sense for the two of you.

But let's say you can't agree and do fight it out in court, or you just want to know how a judge would decide things if you can't work it out. Then the judge will make a decision based on the rules of your state. These rules can be summarized as follows:

- The property each spouse brought into the marriage is considered that spouse's separate property, which that spouse gets to take out of the marriage. For example, if you entered your marriage owning a sport utility vehicle, you get to take it with you when you divorce.

- Similarly, the property a spouse inherited during the marriage is considered that spouse's separate property, which that spouse gets to take out of the marriage. For example, if your great uncle died last year and left you $5,000, the $5,000 is yours and yours alone, as long as you didn't mix it beyond recognition with money belonging to your spouse or jointly owned. If you did, then the entire pool will be considered joint property.

- Property acquired during the marriage and the income earned during the marriage are generally considered marital, or joint, property. In the nine community property states—Arizona, California, Idaho, Louisiana, Nevada, New Mexico, Texas, Washington and Wisconsin—this property, called community property, is divided 50-50. The rest of the states use a property division principle called equitable distribution. There, the property is divided fairly. Often that is 50-50, but sometimes the higher wage earner is given 60% to 75% of the property.

No matter who decides how the property will be divided—you and your spouse or a judge—often, one spouse keeps more property than the other and agrees to make up the difference by making one or more cash payments. These payments are sometimes paid over time. More often, the money is paid down the road a few months or even years in a lump sum after the sale of a house or other valuable asset. This agreement works well in theory, but if you're the one expecting payments, make sure your divorce agreement doesn't leave you vulnerable.

For example, your ex might not make the payments, perhaps out of spite or perhaps because of the lack of money due to a layoff or illness. How will you collect? Sue your ex? Hire a collection agency? Try to reopen your divorce case?

Perhaps you had the foresight to have your ex sign a promissory note (secured by some property your ex keeps, such as the house) agreeing to pay you. If your ex doesn't pay, at least you'd get your share when your ex sells the house or refinances it. But what happens if your ex files for bankruptcy and asks that the promissory note be wiped out? You may be able to protect yourself in advance by specifying in your divorce agreement that the payments are made "in lieu of" alimony or child support-neither of which can be wiped out in bankruptcy. Or, you might be able to protect yourself by including a "hold harmless" agreement in your divorce agreement that essentially prohibits your spouse from wiping out the debt in bankruptcy. Unfortunately for you, neither of these is foolproof, in which case you'd probably have to spend the time and money fighting the bankruptcy case in court, trying to convince a judge that the detriment to you would outweigh any benefit your ex would get by wiping out the debt. Don't count on winning.

There's only one sure way to protect yourself: cash in hand at the time of the divorce. If your ex will pay you out of the sale proceeds of an asset, wait until the sale is final, take the money and then finalize your divorce.

Dividing Debts

Allocating debts can be just as tricky, with a similar set of rules. Again, you can allocate your debts anyway you want. A judge will apply your state rules only if you can't agree on your own and ask a judge to settle the matter. Then, the following rules will apply:

- Each spouse is responsible for paying his or her separate debts brought into the marriage. If you had a student loan from before you got married, for instance, you take it with you at divorce, even if your spouse was paying it off during your marriage.

- Debts incurred after separation but before the divorce is final are generally the responsibility of the spouse who incurred them and must be paid by that person. But both spouses are responsible for paying for family necessities, such as food, shelter and the care of the children.

- In most states, a spouse is responsible for paying only the debts that he or she incurred during a marriage, that is, you can't be forced to pay the bills your spouse runs up, unless they were incurred on a joint account. Then both spouses are fully liable for paying the bills. The rule is different in community property states. There, both spouses are generally liable for all debts incurred during the marriage, unless the creditor was looking to only one spouse for repayment. In community property states, a married person filling out a credit card or loan application alone is asked to indicate his or her marital status. If you check off "married" and don't assertively state something like, "but I intend that this be my separate debt and I, alone, am responsible for this account," then the creditor has the right to go after both spouses for payment, even though the account is in just one person's name. This means that all community property and both spouse's separate property might be at risk of being grabbed to pay all community debts incurred by either spouse.

Your divorce agreement doesn't change your existing obligations to your creditors. So even if your ex agrees to pay the bills as a part of your divorce settlement or was ordered to do so in a divorce decree signed by a judge, the agreement or decree is binding on you and your ex alone. If your ex gets laid off or refuses to pay, the creditors will come after you for payment. If you refuse to pay on the grounds that the debts "belong" to your ex-spouse, your credit will be damaged and the creditors may sue you. You might even have to file bankruptcy. If you do pay the bills, your only remedy is try and get your ex to reimburse you. In rare instances, you might find a judge who would reopen your divorce settlement or decree to award you a greater degree of property, but even so, good luck finding your ex-spouse in order to actually get the property.

If your ex files for bankruptcy to wipe out the debts, you could raise in the bankruptcy court the kinds of objections described in the property section, above. If the judge grants the bankruptcy, you too, might be forced to file.

Again, the advice is simple: sever financial ties if you can, especially regarding debts. Don't divide them. Pay them off. Sell assets (including the house) to take care of the bills. File for bankruptcy jointly before your divorce is final if you have absolutely no other option. If getting rid of the debts isn't possible, then you should agree to pay them in exchange for keeping a greater amount of the marital property. Only as a last resort should you agree to let your spouse pay the debts. You can't be sure he or she will. If this is your only choice, be sure to have your agreement reviewed by a lawyer with expertise in both family law and bankruptcy law who can make the agreement as foolproof as possible. But remember that nothing is guaranteed. Keep your fingers crossed and hope your ex makes good on the obligations.

Divorce Checklist

❏ Close all joint accounts as soon as you become separated or before, if you think separation is imminent and your spouse is continuing to use the card. Remember, you will almost certainly be responsible for any expenses incurred by your spouse during this time.

Just cutting up your card and tossing it in the trash does not close your credit card account. The safest way to close a credit card account is by sending a certified letter, return receipt requested to the customer service department of the card issuer. Ask the card issuer to close your account and to report your account to credit bureaus as "closed by consumer." You can close your account even if you haven't paid off the balance—the card issuer will close your account but still send you your monthly statements until you pay it off in full. In approximately ten days, the card issuer should send you a letter confirming that your account is "closed by the consumer." If you don't receive the confirmation letter, follow up by calling the card issuer to make sure it closed your card and is reporting it properly to the credit bureaus. You may even want to get another copy of your credit report to make sure it is reported correctly.

- ❑ Close all open but unused joint accounts as soon as possible in the method described above. Make sure that you clearly state why you are asking for the account to be closed and that it not be opened again as a joint account. If you are unsure which accounts may be open, order a consolidated copy of your credit report.

- ❑ If possible, continue to keep current on your bills while you are arranging which spouse will be responsible for which bill. Remember that any joint account that your spouse agreed to pay and fails to pay will go on your credit report. You may consider agreeing to pay debts your spouse incurred on credit cards in your name or on joint accounts to protect your credit rating.

- ❑ Don't count on the divorce decree to determine which spouse will pay joint debts; when you have a joint account with your spouse, both you and your spouse are responsible for all joint debts, regardless of how the decree divides the debts. Don't be misled into thinking your spouse is now the only one responsible since he or she "promised to pay."

- ❑ When dividing the debts with your spouse, try to avoid giving your spouse any debt that you are solely responsible for. If he or she defaults on the debt, you are the only one that will suffer.

- ❑ Try to establish credit in your own name. If you are employed and have good credit, apply for a credit card in your own name.

- ❑ If you own jointly held real estate, you should consult with a real estate attorney to find out the best way to get the real estate in your name only.

- ❑ In case of emergency, you can try to pay off debts by selling assets.

- ❑ Get a copy of your credit report and remove any accounts that were in your spouse's name only.

- ❑ If your spouse fails to make payments as arranged, send a statement, 100 words or less, to the credit bureaus explaining the situation. Ask to have it attached to your credit report. Future creditors will be able to better understand why the payments were not made. However, that does not excuse the missed payments.

- ❑ Establish a bank account before the separation in your name only. If the other spouse abuses a bank account, such as bouncing checks on a joint account, this will make it difficult for you to open a new bank account under your name.

CHAPTER 23

What to Do if You Are Sued

Finding yourself at the wrong end of a lawsuit can be very stressful. If you are sued in small claims court, you will find that the system is designed for people who are not necessarily familiar with the court system or its procedures. Often, court rules are relaxed and courts assume the people involved in the lawsuit don't know anything about how the court works. Usually, cases are usually heard by a judge within 30-60 days and disputed amounts are not more than $10,000. In fact, in many states, lawyers are not allowed to be involved in small claims cases, making the court truly a "people's court." A good reference book to use to learn more about small claims court is *Everybody's Guide to Small Claims Court* by Ralph Warner. A copy of the book can be obtained from the online bookstore at www.GetOutOfDebt.org.

For claims involving more money, a creditor would normally sue you in a civil court in your state.

Filing of a Lawsuit

Most court cases begin by the filing of a paper or pleading typically referred to as the Complaint, Petition or Statement of Claim, by the person beginning the lawsuit, usually called the Plaintiff or Complainant. In small claims court, the complaint generally consists of several blank lines on a form, provided by the court, where the Plaintiff can explain why he thinks someone owes him money and how much money should be paid, called "damages."

The complaint in regular civil court is usually more formal. In the complaint, you will find the name of the person or agency who is suing you, your name along with anyone else who may also be named as a responsible party, the date the lawsuit was filed in court, the name of the court, the reason you are being sued and what sort of relief the person suing you wants. The Plaintiff then files the pleading with the court, generally paying a filing fee.

Where the Lawsuit Will Be Filed

Most states have laws that require that people can only be sued in a place where they have "minimum contacts." You will usually be sued either in the county where you live or the state where the problem occurred if you have a substantial connection with that state. Some states only allow a person to be sued in the state where they live.

Service of Process

The court clerk will usually give the pleading a number, and an original copy of the pleading must be served on, or given to, the person being sued, usually called the Defendant or Respondent. A defendant to a lawsuit can receive a copy of the complaint either by certified mail, Sheriff or a private process server. A summons will probably be attached to the complaint, stating the name and address of the person to be served.

Answering the Complaint

If you are served with a complaint in small claims court, it is a good idea to file an answer to the complaint. In many states, answering a small claims lawsuit merely requires that the Defendant sign the pleading and return it to the court. In other states, the Defendant writes an informal letter or pleading. Answering a complaint lets the judge know that you are concerned about resolving the issues raised in the complaint. In most states, however, you will still have a chance to tell the judge your side of the dispute at the small claims hearing, even if you do not file an answer to the complaint.

In regular civil court, if you do not file an answer, a default judgment will probably be entered against you. After a default judgment is entered, most states give you 30 days in which to file an answer after which the judgment becomes final. Once a judgment becomes final, the party who sued can take action to collect the money he or she was awarded.

To answer a complaint, you generally need to admit or deny each numbered statement made in the complaint. In most states, you must raise certain defenses to a lawsuit in your answer or the court will assume you waive those defenses. You will probably need to consult an attorney in your state for help in answering a complaint so that you properly raise any defenses that may benefit you.

Hearings

On a particular day, called the hearing date, the case will be heard by a judge. Usually it is not necessary for you to hire a lawyer to represent you in small claims court. Both sides will be given the opportunity to explain their sides of the dispute to the judge and to present any evidence, such as contracts or statements, to support their arguments. The judge will probably be more likely to consider your point of view if you act in a calm, organized manner. Negative comments or outbursts will make your side of the dispute seem less believable.

If the hearing date falls on a day that is particularly inconvenient, you have a few options. You can contact the party suing you to ask them to agree to change the date. Secondly, you can file a "motion for continuance" (asking the judge to have the hearing at a later time) with the court along with an order for the judge to sign. Finally, you can go to court on the hearing date and ask the judge to postpone the hearing until a later date. If you opt for the third choice, you should realize that the judge may not grant the extension and may go forward with the hearing as scheduled.

Post-Judgment

If the judge decides that the creditor who sued you deserves to be paid, a judgment will be entered against you. If you do not immediately pay the amount of the judgment, the creditor who has the judgment (called a judgment creditor) will have several choices about how to get the money from you.

1. **Wage Garnishment**

    The judgment creditor can ask the court to issue papers, sometimes called a Writ of Garnishment, to be given to your employer with instructions about withholding part of your salary. The employer may send the money directly to the person you owe money to or send it to the court clerk for disbursal. For example, if the amount of the judgment against you was $1,000, your boss may withhold $100 of your salary every month and send it to the judgment creditor until the full $1,000 is paid off. Garnishments may last for a specific amount of time, such as three years, or until the debt is repaid, depending on your state's laws. Your state law will also control how much the creditor can garnish. Generally, the most your creditor can garnish is 25 percent of your disposable income.

    If you do not want your wages to be garnished, you can try to negotiate with the judgment creditor. Sometimes a judgment creditor will be willing to give you the opportunity to make payments directly to him rather than having your wages garnished, with the understanding that if you default in your payments, your wages will be garnished.

2. **Garnishment of Bank Accounts**

    Judgment creditors can also take property, such as bank accounts, to pay off a judgment. The judgment creditor files papers with the court clerk and a court order is then given to your bank. Money you may have in your bank account is given to the judgment creditor to help pay off the amount you owe. If there is not enough money in your account to pay off the debt, other property may be taken and sold to pay the difference or wages can be garnished. Often, a judgment creditor will get another court order at a later time to remove more money from the account if the original amount taken was not enough to repay the debt in full.

3. **Attachment of Personal Property**

    Another means for a judgment creditor to get money from you to repay your debt is taking property that you own and selling it. A judgment creditor can get a court order, called a Writ of Attachment, allowing your property to be taken by the Sheriff. The Sheriff comes to your home with the court order, takes the item specified and places it in storage. If you do not file an objection within a certain time period, the item is sold at a Sheriff's sale. The money received from the sale is used to pay what you owe. If the proceeds of the sale do not cover the amount you owe, you will still be responsible to pay the difference.

    If the Sheriff comes while you are not at home, the law allows him to take the property identified in the Writ of Attachment that is visible without entering any locked spaces. For instance, the Sheriff can take a car sitting idle in the driveway by using a copy of a key or by hotwiring the car. However, if the car is in a locked garage, the Sheriff may not take it. Any property inside your house is also off-limits, unless the Sheriff has a special court order to enter. In this situation, it would be a good idea to allow the Sheriff to enter, rather than to resist.

    If your property has been taken and you are able to pay the amount of the judgment, you can offer to make the payment in exchange for the return of your property.

Satisfaction of Judgment

Once you have paid off a judgment, a wise debtor will always ask for a document that shows that the judgment has been paid in full (called a satisfaction of judgment). This document will serve as proof for any later transaction where you need to prove the debt has been paid. This document will come in handy if your credit report does not show the judgment satisfied. If it doesn't, send a copy of the satisfaction of judgment to each of the credit bureaus that are reporting it incorrectly and ask them to update their records.

To Research this Topic Further:

Procedures relating to small claims cases vary per state. If you are sued in small claims court, often the court designated on the complaint will have brochures or printed information for consumers. You can also research issues using the law library at your local courthouse. Ask the librarian to direct you to your state code and to the place where local laws or ordinances are kept. Use the index to find your topic. Your state code will contain statutes or state laws that apply to your situation. Most state codes have annotations, which show how the judges in your state have interpreted a law on a case-by-case basis. Be sure to check the updates to any volume of the state code or local laws you are looking in. Updates contain important information regarding any changes to the law that have occurred.

It may also be helpful to contact an attorney in your state for legal advice. To locate an attorney, you can call the bar association in your state and ask whether it offers a lawyer referral service. If all else fails, attorneys are listed alphabetically in the yellow pages.

"The paper and ink content is within acceptable norms, but the contract itself appears to have too many clauses."

CHAPTER 24

Stuck in a Contract: What to Do Before and After You Sign Up for Clubs

Whether you're planning an excursion to the Virgin Islands, negotiating a timeshare in Vermont, or thinking about getting into shape by joining a health club, the contract you sign will determine the rules you will have to follow throughout the entire term of the contract. Reading carefully before you sign will help you to avoid problems later. Generally, if you change your mind, you have three days to cancel the contract.

Health Clubs

Choosing a Health Club

A health club is a facility where people can go to improve their physical condition or appearance through exercise. Often, consumers get lured by high pressure sales tactics into signing a contract without considering whether or not they are able to make the time and financial commitments. Before signing a contract to join a health club, read the contract carefully. Pay particular attention to the cancellation and refund provisions and make sure you understand the duration of the contract. Before deciding to join, it is wise to tour the facility you are considering so you can see the type of equipment and classes offered.

Check to see if:

- The hours of operation and location are convenient for you.
- The equipment is well-maintained.
- The club limits the number of future members to avoid overcrowding.
- The instructors are qualified.

- The club limits hours of use (for example, men only or women only at certain times).
- The club has met state regulations, such as proper licensing.
- The cost of the club is affordable.
- The atmosphere seems friendly with staff willing to help you learn how to use the equipment.
- The club makes realistic representations about the results you can expect to obtain.

Remember that if a problem arises after you join a club, the contract will govern how the problem is resolved. If items are missing from the contract and there is a problem, it probably will not be easily resolved.

Contract Considerations

Read through the entire contract before signing anything. Make sure the contract lists all the services and facilities and determine if any services require additional fees. See if the contract allows you to use other facility locations at no charge. Think about the term of the contract. Will you really use the club for two years or would it be better to sign up one year at a time? (In most states, a health club contract may not exceed three years.) Better still, negotiate with the club to allow you to try the facility for a short time. A trial membership allows you to visit the club at peak hours to see how crowded the club may become.

Make sure you fully understand exactly how much you will be required to pay and in what increments (all up front or monthly). Ask whether the fee you have been quoted includes an enrollment fee and any finance charges. Often you can negotiate with the club to eliminate initiation fees.

When you join a health club, the club should give you a copy of the contract. The contract should contain:

- The name and address of the health club.
- The date the contract was signed.
- A full description of the club's equipment and services, including the date any future equipment or services will be available for use. Any future services or equipment should be available within 12 months of when the contract was signed, unless there are extenuating circumstances.
- The total cost including initiation and membership fees, and whether or not these fees can be raised. Most states have a limit as to how often the dues can be raised each year.
- Information about your cancellation and refund rights.

Cancellation and Refund Policies

The vast majority of problems with health club contracts arise as a result of disputes regarding cancellation and refund rights. In most states, you have the right to cancel your membership for any reason within three days after signing a contract, called a cooling-off period. (Do not include legal holidays or Sundays when calculating the three-day period.) Cancellations should be in writing, preferably sent by certified, return receipt requested mail so you have proof of delivery. The club must refund your money within 30 days after receiving your written cancellation notice. The cancellation letter must usually be postmarked by midnight of the third day. If you elect to hand-deliver the notice to the club, ask the manager to initial and date the notice and keep a copy for your records. The club generally should give you a prorated refund of your initiation fee. However, if you signed a separate clause stating that the initiation fee is non-refundable, you are probably not entitled to any money back, and you may be responsible to pay the rest of your initiation fee. You probably will not be obligated, after properly canceling your membership, to continue to make payments, unless you financed the initiation fee and signed a non-refundable clause. In that case, you will still need to make payments until you have paid the initiation fee in full.

Often, you can cancel a contract if it is for greater than one year, and you move more than 25 miles from the health club, and the club does not have an affiliation with a club within 25 miles of your new home offering the same services at no additional charge. You are often entitled to a full refund where the club fails to provide equipment and services promised by the date specified in the contract. For example, the contract states that the club will have aerobics classes every half-hour and will be getting six new stationary bicycles by a certain date. The date passes and you discover that the club only offers aerobics classes once a week. In some states you would be entitled to a full refund.

Most states require that you receive a refund when the health club closes permanently and the owner does not own a comparable facility within ten miles of the club. You would most likely be entitled to a prorated refund of your initiation fee.

The membership can usually be cancelled upon death or total and sometimes partial disability of the consumer. If the contract says part of the initiation fee is non-refundable, the non-refundable portion can be subtracted out from the prorated refund. Prorated refunds are generally calculated by dividing the contract price by the total number of weeks in your membership and multiplying the result by the number of weeks remaining in your membership.

Health clubs cannot automatically renew your membership when the contract is over without getting your permission. The club must wait until the end of your membership before signing you up again, assuming you want to renew the membership. Before purchasing a health club membership, you may want to contact the consumer affairs office in your state to find out whether there are any state laws about health clubs that may affect you.

Common Problems with Health Clubs

- High pressure sales tactics that intimidate people into purchasing memberships they may not have opted to buy. For example, a salesperson may cause a consumer to join by having him fill out a long contract after coming into the club out of curiosity to take a look around, thus making the consumer feel guilty that the salesperson did all that work.

- Misrepresentations about the facility's equipment, staff or services

- Offering low-cost trial memberships only to try to pressure consumers into buying more expensive memberships when they use the low cost plan, and

- Pre-opening memberships that don't open on the date specified. In most states, you are entitled to a full refund of your initiation fee if the club does not open on the date specified. Generally, you can also cancel the contract within the first five days the facility is open if you are not satisfied.

What if You Want to Get Out of Your Contract?

Getting out of a health club contract can be quite difficult, unless laws have somehow been broken. Your best bet is to contact the health club, explain that you desire to end the contract and request that the contract be terminated. Your chances of success will be greater if you can give specific reasons for your request, such as loss of a job rendering you financially unable to make payments or health problems making it impossible for you to use the gym. Look at the contract you signed to see if it allows you to pay a penalty for breaking the contract rather than holding you accountable for payment for the rest of the contract term.

Many people join a health club with the best of intentions only to find themselves trapped in a contract for a club they have become dissatisfied with. Be an informed consumer before you enter an agreement you may be stuck with for a long time. Remember that if a problem arises after you join a club, the contract will govern how the problem is resolved. Make sure it is a contract you can live with.

Timeshare Clubs

As an alternative to purchasing a vacation home, many consumers have entered into timeshare agreements. For a lump sum, usually several thousand dollars, the consumer obtains the rights to use a specific property for a certain number of weeks per year. As with other types of clubs, before entering into an agreement that will bind you, you need to understand the fine print.

After identifying the particular timeshare you are interested in, contact the Consumer Affairs and/or Consumer Protection Division in the state where the property is located to see if any complaints have been registered. The Real Estate Commission in the state where the property may be found generally regulates timesharing.

In reviewing the terms of the contract, consider:

- **Costs.** Make sure the contract identifies all costs involved, including maintenance fees and taxes, closing costs, finance charges, commissions and any other miscellaneous charges. Ask whether any fees are subject to increase each year and, if so, whether there is an established maximum that the fees may be increased. Check with a few hotels in the area in which the timeshare is located to see whether their prices are comparable to that of the timeshare. This will also help you to negotiate a fair price if you decide to purchase the timeshare.

- **Cooling-off Period.** Most states allow for a period of time where the consumer can change his mind with no penalty. Make sure your contract specifically provides for a period of time where you can cancel the contract and receive a refund. Specify whether the cancellation must be in writing.

- **Terms.** Make sure the contract includes promises made by the seller that may not have been in writing.

- **Cancellation/Refund Clause.** If at all possible, try to include a clause in the contract that allows you to terminate the contractual relationship if you decide at a later time you no longer wish to participate. Try to preserve your right to cancel at any time rather than only for a specified amount of time. For example, include a clause that allows you to cancel the contract after thirty-days notice at any time rather than a statement that cancellation must occur within the first year, if at all.

- **Trading Facilities.** If you are interested in being able to arrange trades in other locations, make sure the contract specifically allows for that. Any associated costs should be clearly stated.

Before signing a contract, consider whether you will be able to make use of the timeshare over time. Timeshares usually require that you use the timeshare property at the same time each year for the same length of time. Therefore, you may not have the luxury of vacationing at a different season or for a different length of time. If the timeshare is far from your home, you will need to spend money travelling to get there which may become costly year after year. Even if you are ill or cannot travel to the timeshare for whatever reason, you will probably still be responsible financially for the costs outlined in your contract.

Getting Out of Your Timeshare Agreement

Your first step in trying to end a contractual relationship is to review the provisions you have agreed to in the contract. Look for a clause allowing cancellation. Next, find out whether your state has enacted any laws that may be of help in canceling the contract. Many states have laws regarding timeshare arrangements. Ask if you can pay a penalty rather than paying the full amount of the entire term of the contract.

Campground/Travel Club Memberships

Often consumers are lured into considering the purchase of a travel club or campground membership after receiving an unsolicited letter in the mail stating that they have been specially selected to win a prize. A list of possible prizes are generally named, including a high-price item such as a car or boat. Usually, consumers are instructed to contact the resort to make an appointment to claim their prize. Once they contact the resort, consumers learn that there are certain "eligibility" requirements to claim the prize. Consumers are asked to give information about their employment, salary range and credit. Often, even after viewing the resort, prizes are either not awarded if a membership is not purchased or are of a different quality than that represented in the solicitation.

In this short scenario, a host of violations of a law called the Unfair and Deceptive Acts and Practices have occurred. Rather than being "specially selected," the recipients of these letters are chosen at random from mail order houses. A resort may not require a consumer to purchase a membership in order to receive a promised prize. Likewise, the resort may not misrepresent that the prize is of a certain value or fail to disclose the odds of winning a particular prize. Usually, a large, expensive prize is not awarded by each particular resort, but rather, by the greater industry. Remember that an announcement that you have been "selected to receive" a club membership or vacation does not mean that it will be free.

The Sales Presentation

Upon visiting the resort, the consumer will probably be given a tour and told that the resort is authorized to allow the consumer to purchase a membership for a much lower price than the average person since he or she has been "specially selected." However, the consumer is warned, the reduced price may only be offered on that particular day and will be withdrawn after the consumer leaves the resort. Legitimate companies generally do not expect a consumer to make a quick decision without allowing time to carefully consider an offer. During the sales presentation, it is unlawful for resorts to:

- ■ Continually try to convince the consumer to purchase a membership even when it becomes apparent that the consumer is unable to afford the initial cost or subsequent payments.
- ■ Trap the consumer for long periods of time to give a very long sales pitch.
- ■ Misrepresent the current facilities or future improvements planned.

- Ask for or accept postdated checks or a credit card knowing that the consumer did not have sufficient funds or credit to cover the payment.
- State that only a few memberships are left, if that is untrue.
- Insist that the consumer participate in events aimed at promoting the sale of a membership to receive a promised prize.
- Pretend to offer certain special discounts for one day only or to certain groups, such as newlyweds, when the price is the same regardless of the day or people involved.

Contract Considerations

After the tour, a consumer who desires to purchase a travel or campground membership may be expecting to receive information regarding the terms and conditions of the sale. Instead, the resort employee may give the consumer merely an agreement to purchase the membership with little details about the actual benefits of the membership. At this stage, consumers should expect the contract to contain:

- A statement of the total price, including down payment and any extra costs;
- Information about how to cancel the contract;
- A clause allowing both the resort and the consumer to cancel the contract;
- Obligations and duties owed by both the resort to the member and the member to the resort;
- Detailed information regarding whether the consumer is permitted to use other facilities, amenities included; and
- A statement about whether the membership is transferable or assignable.

Consumers should be wary of contracts which include:

- A statement that the consumer will forfeit all monies paid in the event the consumer defaults.
- Forms which are notarized at the resort (consumers should realize that even contracts that are notarized may be cancelled).
- References to other documents which are not attached and the consumer has not had the opportunity to read (for example, a section which may refer to "the attached plan" or "attachment A" which is not included in the contract given to the consumer).
- Statements that the contract cannot be cancelled at any time.

Practical Suggestions

Before entering into a travel or campground membership, consumers should weigh the likelihood of continued use of the membership together with the on-going financial obligation. Next listen carefully to the sales presentation for specific details about the membership. If the membership is for a travel club, get the names of hotels, airlines and restaurants included in your package.

Do not accept vague statements that the package includes "all major hotels and/or airlines" or you may be quite disappointed with the quality of the services you are offered. Finally, do not sign the agreement until you have received and read all documents. Once you sign, it is extremely difficult to get out of the agreement unless the resort has acted improperly. You can try contacting the membership office and explaining that you wish to cancel your contract. Hopefully, the contract includes a clause that allows you to end the contract without paying the full contract price. If not, ask about the possibility of paying a penalty rather than the full price.

Common Threads in All Types of Contracts

First and foremost, **DO NOT SIGN A CONTRACT WITHOUT READING IT!** Remember that the terms of the contract will govern disputes that arise. Be an informed consumer before you agree to sign up. If you are not sure about certain details, do not hesitate to ask for more information in writing. If you have agreed to terms that you become unable to meet, you will most likely still have to pay. Think about the term of the contract—if it is for a long time, decide whether you will be able to meet the financial and health requirements to participate for years to come. A cancellation clause will be your greatest help in your effort to cancel the contract. If your contract does not contain a cancellation clause and nothing illegal has transpired, chances are you're STUCK!

If you feel your rights have been violated or you have been treated unfairly, there are several sources to assist you. Draft a detailed letter outlining the circumstances and explaining how you feel you have been treated improperly. Send a copy of the letter to the other party indicating that copies have also been sent to the Federal Trade Commission, the Consumer Protection Agency and the Better Business Bureau. Hopefully, either this will entice the other party to be more cooperative in resolving the problem or you will receive needed help from these organizations. Finally, find out whether your state has enacted any laws that may help. Club memberships have been a topic of discussion among several lawmakers and several states have enacted laws aimed at helping the consumer.

CHAPTER 25

Child Support: Answers to Commonly Asked Questions

Parents have an obligation to financially support their children, whether the parents are married or divorced. Children, likewise, have the right to be supported. Often, when parents decide to separate, courts require the parent who does not have custody of the children to pay a monthly amount to the parent who has custody to help offset expenses associated with the child's day-to-day needs. This amount is called **child support** or **maintenance**. As a part of child support, a non-custodial parent may also be required by the court to pay health insurance, childcare expenses and education costs for the child. Many people are in debt and are having financial problems because they are not receiving child support payments. Being informed about the rules and regulations regarding child support can help.

How Much Child Support Does the Spouse Who Does Not Have Custody Have to Pay?

Most states have established guidelines for determining the amount of support that children are entitled to receive. The guidelines are a set of rules and tables for calculating the amount of child support a parent should pay. Usually, the amount to be paid is based upon the income the non-custodial spouse earns each month in relation to how many children are to be supported. Some parents are able to agree on the amount of child support while others require the help of the court to set a support amount. Courts often have sample forms to help calculate the amount of child support a non-custodial parent will be required to pay.

Can the Child Support Amount Be Changed After the Court Gives an Order?

The person who wants the support amount to be changed usually needs to be able to show that circumstances have changed since the court order was entered. For example, suppose the non-custodial spouse held a full-time job at the time of the child support hearing and an amount of support was determined. Later, the person became a part-time worker due to company cutbacks. He or she may be able to request that the judge reduce the amount of child support based upon changed circumstances. Other possible circumstances that a judge may decide are significant include new medical expenses, disability of the non-custodial parent, educational expenses or a large increase in salary of either parent. The judge may also consider modifying a support order if the child begins to spend significantly more time with the non-custodial parent than when the court initially ordered the support.

Can I Prohibit the Non-Custodial Parent From Visiting My Child Because Child Support Has Not Been Properly Paid?

Child support and visitation are considered separate issues. Usually, even if the non-custodial parent has not met the child support obligation, the parent is still entitled to visit with the child. By the same token, a parent who is denied visitation must still pay child support. If you try to stop the non-custodial parent from visiting with the child because he or she did not pay child support, you may be sued.

What if the Non-Custodial Parent Remarries? Can the New Spouse's Income Be Considered Toward the Child Support Award?

Since the new spouse does not have an obligation to support the child, the additional income usually cannot be considered as available for child support. However, it is possible that the court will assume that the non-custodial parent now must pay less of his/her own expenses and that more of the non-custodial parent's salary will be considered available for child support.

If the Non-Custodial Parent Begins a New Family and Has Other Children to Support, Will the Amount of Child Support Owed to the Original Child Be Reduced?

Because someone becomes the parent of other children does not relieve him or her from the obligation to support the original child. The non-custodial parent may try to request that the support order be modified due to changed circumstances—the obligation to support additional children. The judge will decide if the new circumstances warrant a reduction in child support but will rarely relieve the person of the obligation to support the original child.

What if the Non-Custodial Parent Declares Bankruptcy?

Child support payments are not dischargeable in bankruptcy. The parent who must pay child support is obligated to pay for the time agreed or stated in the order. The only exception may be where a modification of child support has been made.

If the Non-Custodial Parent Refuses to Pay Child Support as Ordered, Is It a Crime?

In most states, failure to support your child is a crime. Many states have court-ordered "round-ups" of parents who owe support. These parents may be jailed until the amount owed is paid. Similarly, a parent who refuses to get a job or voluntarily impoverishes himself or herself may be given the choice of getting a job by a certain date or becoming incarcerated in some states.

What Can the State Do to Help if Child Support Is Not Paid as Ordered by the Court?

Someone who refuses to pay court-ordered child support would be in contempt of court if he/she fails to pay. Many states have established a division of the State's Attorney Office (sometimes called the Office of Child Support Enforcement) devoted exclusively to child support issues. When someone does not pay as ordered by the court, the State may be able to attach the wages or bank account of the non-paying parent, intercept any tax refund that may be owed or place a lien on personal and real property belonging to that parent. Money from these sources is often paid to the court who then distributes the money to the custodial parent. Usually, the custodial parent does not have to pay for these services. If there is no court order, it will probably not be possible to obtain income from these sources, unless the non-custodial parent agrees to allow these resources to be used.

What Happens if I Know Who the Father of the Child Is but He Denies It Because He Does Not Want to Pay Child Support?

Most states have approved the use of paternity tests to determine whether an individual is the parent of a particular child. The test involves taking a minimal blood sample from both the alleged parent and the child. A paternity hearing is held at which paternity may be established. Aside from genetic testing, a court will usually consider other factors such as: resemblance of the alleged father and child, acknowledgment of paternity at the time of the birth by signing the child's birth certificate, or voluntarily support payments sent by the alleged father.

What if I Ended on Good Terms With the Non-Custodial Parent and Don't Want to "Rock The Boat" by Asking for Child Support (or I Never Want to Have Anything to Do With That Jerk Again!)?

Since the payment is a result of the child's right to be supported, rather than the custodial parent's right to receive the support, a custodial parent usually would not be able to waive a child's right to support. Children have the right to be supported by their parents in all states.

Can the State Suspend the Driver's License of a Parent Who Ignores a Court Order to Pay Child Support?

In many states, suspension of a driver's license is allowed to enforce an order of child support. The person is often notified by mail that the license is about to be suspended. Sometimes, the person is given a period of time, usually 30 days, to clear up the past amount owed before the license will actually be suspended.

What Should I Do if the Non-Custodial Parent Refuses to Pay Child Support?

You can contact the Child Support Enforcement agency in your state. Usually, the State's Attorney Office will bring suit to enforce court-ordered support and the custodial parent does not pay for these services. Also, there are several non-profit organizations designed to help custodial parents recover child support payments. Many private agencies have begun to offer child support recovery services as well, often charging an application fee. Usually these companies keep a percentage of what is collected on behalf of the custodial parent. Be sure you understand all charges and fees before signing up with the agency.

Can the Non-Custodial Parent Avoid Paying Court-Ordered Child Support by Moving Out of State?

The obligation to pay child support does not end because a parent moves out of state. The federal government and each state maintains a parent locator service. Parents who owe support may be found through use of federal, state and local records. Federal sources include the IRS and Social Security records. States can research records relating to motor vehicles, unemployment and public entitlements (i.e. welfare). Local records may involve a review of tax or library records. Credit reports may be another useful source since arrearages of more than $1,000 will probably be reported to the credit bureau. It is generally not permissible to use census records to locate parents who owe child support.

Can the Non-Custodial Parent Be Publicly Humiliated Into Paying Court-Ordered Child Support?

Certainly, within reason. Often child support enforcement agencies will post the name of a person who has defaulted on child support payments on a "most wanted" list which may be published and circulated or made into a poster and hung in a prominent place. Some states allow the name of the debtor to appear on cable television on hundreds of occasions or to take out a full-page advertisement in a local newspaper on a regular basis. A review of many Internet sites reveals stories accompanied by pictures of a parent who has failed to pay court-ordered child support. Often these stories include a picture of the child who is suffering due to the failure of the non-custodial parent to pay child support. It would be wise to consult an attorney before attempting the public humiliation tactic yourself.

When Does the Obligation to Pay Child Support End?

Usually, a court order requiring a parent to pay child support will state the date upon which the obligation will cease. Likewise, any agreement entered into by both parents should include a termination date. If no date is specified, depending on what your state's laws are, usually the obligation to pay child support continues until the child reaches the age of majority or possibly, until they finish college. If the child is disabled, the obligation may continue until the child is able to become independent.

Remember that the child has a legal right to receive child support. Support obligations are usually enforced to the fullest extent of the law. Unfortunately, due to the number of non-custodial parents who fail to pay child support, child support enforcement agencies are overflowing with cases. Be persistent and do not let your case inadvertently "slip through the cracks." Receipt of the child support that your child is owed may make the difference between becoming hopelessly in debt and the ability to pay your bills. There are a multitude of resources available to help. Become familiar with your state's laws regarding child support and the enforcement of court-ordered support. If you are not sure where to begin, start with your state's consumer protection office for guidance.

CHAPTER 26

Bounced Checks: What to Do if You Write Them...or Receive Them

Money's tight, the bills are due and you're expecting a paycheck in a few days. So you write some checks and cross your fingers that they don't hit the bank before your deposit.

Or maybe you're flat broke and figure writing a few rubber checks can't hurt. After all, you figure, those businesses have plenty of money and can just write off the loss.

Or perhaps you didn't mean to write a bad check—you just thought you had more money in your account than you did.

Whatever your reason, writing a bad check can be bad news.

First of all, it can be expensive. You're almost guaranteed your bank will charge you a bad check fee—probably $25 or more. On top of that, the merchant who received the bad check will probably charge you a fee of $25 and can sue you for damages, often up to two or three times the amount of the check. (They'll usually have to give you the chance to make good on the check first.)

Secondly, writing a check when you know you don't have the money to cover it is a crime. According to attorney Robin Leonard, however, if the district attorney decides to prosecute, you may be able to avoid a trial by taking classes—and making good on the checks, of course.

If you have written a bad check, contact the person to whom you wrote it immediately and either pay it or make payment arrangements. Obviously, it's better to prevent the problem in the first place.

A good way to prevent the problem is by signing up for overdraft protection. Although the interest rates on these lines of credit can be rather high, it's usually much cheaper than the fees that pile up if the check doesn't clear.

If you do bounce a check, that fact may be reported to a check verification company (similar to a credit reporting company) and may make it more difficult for you to open an account in the future. Ask the merchant if it reports information to a check verification company. If so, ask for the telephone number so you can call and find out what the check verification company has on file about you.

You may also want to ask about your bank's check clearing policy. Some banks, if presented with several checks on the same day, will clear larger checks first, which could mean more bounced checks for you (and more expensive fees for the bank to collect). If this happens to you, and you've never bounced a check before, talk to the bank manager about waiving some of the fees. After all, it only costs the bank somewhere between 50 cents and $1.50 to process a bounced check, but you'll probably pay much more than that in fees.

Check-Writing Tips

- Remember that a check is a personalized form of money. Fill in all information clearly in a form that cannot be altered.

- Always use a pen when filling out a check, never a pencil or a felt-tip marker. Ink from a pen cannot be easily erased or smeared.

- Always use the current date on a check; never postdate it. To avoid alteration, write out the date instead of using numerical abbreviations.

- Put all check information as far to the left on each line as possible. When filling in the written amount, draw a line through any remaining space.

- Avoid using abbreviations on the "pay to the order of" line.

- To ensure legibility, print the written amount of the check; don't write it in cursive.

- Make sure that the written amount is exactly the same as the numerical amount. If the two differ, the written amount is considered legally binding.

- Sign your name neatly; your signature should match the one on file at your bank. Illegible scrawls are easy to forge.

- If you tear a check or make a mistake when filling it out, void the check and write a new one. Remember to list any unusable checks in your check register.

Source: Checkbooklet, Federal Reserve Bank of Boston.

Balancing Your Checkbook

The majority of people who bounce a check believe they have more in their account than is actually there due to an error in recording payments, funds transfers, withdrawls or deposits. Balancing your checkbook monthly can help you catch these errors before they end up costing you a lot of money in bank fees. The following is a step-by-step guide for reconciling your account to the penny.

Step 1   Compare your bank statement to your check register to see if all of your checks have been posted to your account. There should be a place in your register to check off that each check has been posted.

Step 2   Subtract any bank charges that you have not already accounted for in your register, such as ATM fees.

Step 3   Subtract any electronic fund transfers, e.g. car payments, insurance.

Step 4   Add any automatic deposits, such as direct deposit paychecks or dividends that have yet been recorded.

Step 5   Add any interest that your account may have earned.

Step 6   List all of your outstanding checks (checks that have been written but have not yet been cleared by your bank—some checks may not be cashed by the recipient for several months from the time you wrote them). Put this on the reconciliation sheet provided in the bank statement or in the back of your checkbook.

Step 7   Total the amount of outstanding checks.

Step 8   Subtract that amount from what your bank says you have as the ending balance on the bank statement. This is often referred to as the new balance. This usually does not match your actual register.

Step 9   Add any deposits you have made which are not listed on your bank statement.

Step 10   Compare the balance on the reconciliation sheet to the bank statement and your register. These should agree.

Step 11   If they do not agree, try the following:

- Compare register and deposit slips with your statement. You may have forgotten to write something in your register.
- If the error is a whole number, check your addition and subtraction.
- If the error is divisible by nine, numbers may have been transposed.

If the balances still do not agree and you cannot find the problem, visit your bank. A customer relations representative can help you find the problem.

When You're on the Receiving End

Accepting a check that doesn't clear is no fun, either. Many banks these days will charge you—the recipient—a bad check fee. On top of that, you'll have the additional time and cost of trying to collect on it, if it's not fraudulent. (The FBI calls check fraud "the financial crime of the 90s.")

Here are steps you can take to protect yourself from taking a rubber check:

1. Watch out for low number checks (those numbering 101-499). An estimated nine out of ten bad checks fall into this low-number range. You may want to use a check verification service or take additional steps to verify these checks before accepting them. Starter checks may also be troublesome.

2. Look for fakes. Personal checks with four smooth edges (no perforations) or shiny or glossy numbers are worth double-checking—they may be counterfeits printed on laser printers. Take extra precaution with checks where the last three digits or four numbers of the Federal Reserve number at the top of the check (see Field 4 in sample check on the next page) are different from the first three or four numbers at the bottom. (See Field 3 in the sample check). Checks should also have the name of the bank, and usually a location.

3. Protect your rights. Find out from your state attorney general's office or district attorney's office what steps you should take when accepting a check to protect your rights if you need to collect or sue later.

4. Double check identification. Many bad checks are cashed with an expired driver's license. Check the expiration date and compare the signature and address on the license with those on the check.

If you have accepted a bad check, you'll generally have to send a written demand for payment, and the check writer will usually have 30 days to pay. If the check writer doesn't, you may be able to sue for the amount of the check, plus damages.

If you're not sure a check will clear, you may want to take it to the bank where the account is held to cash it. This way you'll avoid a bad check fee from your bank if your suspicions prove true and it bounces.

JAMES C. MORRISON
1765 Sheridan Drive
Balsam Lake, WI 54810
(715) 555-5555

101
79-123/759

Date *July 20, 1999*

PAY TO THE ORDER OF *Payee* $ *392.75*

three hundred ninety-two and 75/100 DOLLARS

Balsam Lake State Bank
Balsam Lake, WI 54810

FOR *example*

James C. Morrison

⑈075901231⑈ 4563271⑊ 0101 ⑈0000039275⑈

Field 3- Routing/Transit Number
Field 2- Customer Account Number
Field 1- Check Number
Field 4- Federal Reserve Number

Elements of a Good Check

One of the most important factors in limiting check fraud losses is education. In order to recognize a fraudulent check, you have to be familiar with the components that make up a good check. The Federal Reserve Bank of Boston recommends that all parties who participate in check transactions should be aware of the following elements of a good check (see the sample check above).

1. **Perforation.** Look for at least one perforated side on most checks.

2. **Federal Reserve District and Office.** The first two digits of the routing/transit number (Field 3) indicate the Federal Reserve District (01-Boston, 02-New York, 03-Philadelphia, 04-Cleveland, 05-Richmond, 06-Atlanta, 07-Chicago, 08-St. Louis, 09-Minneapolis, 10-Kansas city, 11-Dallas, 12-San Francisco). The Federal Reserve District in the sample check is "07." The third digit (in this example, the number "5") indicates the district office.

3. **Bank address.** The address of the bank should correspond to the appropriate Federal Reserve District. For example, if you receive the sample check—from Wisconsin—the routing/transit number depicts the Seventh Federal Reserve District (07). (See Fields 3 and 4)

4. **Bank ID Number.** Positions 5 through 8 of Field 3 identify the issuing bank.

5. **Account Number.** Field 2 identifies the customer's account number.

6. **Serial Number.** Field 1 identifies the serial number or check number. This number should match the check number at the top right corner of the check, in this example, "101."

7. **Fractional Routing/Transit Number.** The denominator of the fraction in Field 4 (in this case, "759") should match the Bank Identification Number in Field 3. On some checks (like the one in this example), there is a zero in front of the Bank ID Number. A few checks may not have fractional numbers listed in Field 4. This does not necessarily mean those checks are fraudulent, but merchants may want to investigate more closely.

Adapted from: *Check Fraud Awareness*, Federal Reserve Bank of Boston.

CHAPTER 27

How Being in Debt Can Affect Your Military Career

Being in the military poses unique problems for military personnel and their families. Sometimes as a result of circumstances, such as relocation or deployment of a spouse, a military member may fall behind on payments of his debts. A person who is behind on payments may be viewed in the military as irresponsible, even when the person fully intends to pay. Thus, finding yourself in debt and in the military could seriously hamper your career plans and goals. Understanding how the military views those in debt may help you to avoid common mistakes and save your career.

How Being in Debt Can Affect Your Career

Generally, people who are in the military have an obligation to pay their "just financial obligations" in a proper and timely manner. Debts are considered "just" when the military member agrees that he owes the debt or the debt has been reduced to a judgment which conforms to the Soldiers' and Sailors' Civil Relief Act (see Chapter 28). You risk either being formally disciplined or even administratively discharged with a loss of benefits if you don't pay your debts and:

- You act deceitfully or lie.
- You commit a fraudulent act.
- You intentionally refuse to pay your debts for reasons other than a lack of funds to do so.

Even if your debts have been discharged in bankruptcy, you can be disciplined for dishonorable failure to pay just debts committed before you filed bankruptcy. The military does not discourage or encourage bankruptcy. However, the reasons you filed for bankruptcy will probably be examined to see if they reflect negatively on your military character. On the other hand, it is unlikely that a military member would be disciplined because he has made some poor financial decisions and finds himself owing more than he can pay without deliberately meaning to do so. In deciding whether to discipline a military member because of his indebtedness, the reason the member is in debt may become quite important.

Being in debt can affect how much responsibility is given to a military member. Usually, the military considers a person in debt to have acted irresponsibly and may find that his failure to pay just debts is a consideration in:

- Obtaining/retaining security clearances.
- Granting an advancement in rate.
- Offering special duty assignments.
- Qualifications for reenlistment or extension of enlistment.
- Determining general character and trustworthiness of the military member.

When the Debt Collector or Creditor Contacts Your Commanding Officer

A person in the military may feel like an easy target for debt collectors and creditors. To collect the debt, the creditor or collector often sends a letter to the debtor's Commanding Officer, called a letter of indebtedness, stating that the individual is behind on his or her payments. The letter is sent on the hope that the Officer will put pressure on the debtor to pay the debt. A recent Virginia Tech study on the financial state of the Navy found that in one year, the Navy processed more than 123,000 letters of indebtedness. Such practices, although widespread, may violate the Fair Debt Collections Practices Act or other laws designed to protect consumers.

Whether it is proper for a Commanding Officer to receive a letter of indebtedness will depend on whether the sender is a debt collector or a creditor. A "debt collector" is someone whose principal business is collecting a debt for another person or business. A "creditor" is a business or person who first extended you credit or loaned you money such as a collection department in retail stores, finance companies or banks.

Generally, if a debt collector contacts a third-party, such as a person's employer, merely to inform that person that the debtor owes a debt, without the permission of the debtor or a court judgment, the collector violates the Fair Debt Collection Practices Act. However, the call will probably be allowed under the Act if the reason the collector is calling the third-party is either:

- To ask the third-party how to locate the debtor; or

- To inform someone who has a legitimate business reason to know about the debt (for example, wage garnishment or alimony).

There may also be related state laws that protect consumers as well.

Contacting the Commanding Officer may often yield little results for the debt collector since the Officer usually has no power to get involved in disputes or enforce agreements between the debtor and the debt collector. Likewise, the Officer usually will not act as a debt collector on behalf of someone trying to collect a debt from a service member.

Certain branches of the military may even have a procedure where letters of indebtedness from debt collectors are returned with no action taken if the correspondence violates the Fair Debt Collection Practices Act or state statutes. The military member could probably sue a debt collector for contacting a Commanding Officer without his permission or a court order under the Act.

Letters of indebtedness sent to a Commanding Officer from *creditors* are not prohibited by the Fair Debt Collection Practices Act. In that case, the only power a Commanding Officer may have over payment of the debt would be to contact the military member and to ensure that the member contacts the creditor in a timely manner to discuss his intentions regarding repayment. The communication to the military member may also include:

- Counseling regarding repayment of debts (such practices as requiring the service member to submit a statement showing his monthly income and detailing how money is spent each month to help the member budget his money more effectively);

- Referral to the legal staff; or

- Referral to military financial counseling.

The Commanding Officer may also review the terms of the debt to ensure that the creditor has met standards of fairness and has complied with federal disclosure requirements under law.

Any requests by the creditor to furnish information about the member's credit rating will probably not be answered by the Commanding Officer. However, the Commanding Officer may release information about the following:

- The member's duty station

- Verification that the member is in the military service

- Duty address
- Basic pay information

What Resources Are Available to Help

Remember that when a service person gets into financial hot water, it could cost him his job. There is help available. Resources include:

- Legal Assistance Offices.
- Military Family Service Centers.
- Military Financial Specialists.

The Soldiers' and Sailors' Civil Relief Act provides protection to members of the military by limiting claims that can be made against them while in military service. Some of these protections involve the following:

- Credit transactions
- Court proceedings
- Statute of limitations
- Evictions

You may want to ask a legal assistance office for help in understanding how the Soldiers' and Sailors' Civil Relief Act may help you. (See Chapter 28.)

Finally, becoming aware of how you spend your finances to avoid becoming deeper in debt may be vital to your job security. Experts cite a variety of reasons military members get into debt including financial scams, loneliness and frequent moves which may cause a working spouse to lose a job. Try to break the cycle of becoming in debt by:

- Getting help from experienced professionals who have dealt with problem debtors such as Debt Counselors of America®.
- Seeking help for the psychological causes of getting into debt to help control your spending.
- Making payments toward lowering your debt without adding to the debt load.
- Educating yourself about smart spending, scams and financial planning.

CHAPTER 28

How the Soldiers' and Sailors' Civil Relief Act Can Help You

Debt Counselors of America has noticed that many servicepersons experience financial difficulties that are unique and need special attention. This chapter will discuss their rights and protections under the Soldiers' and Sailors' Civil Relief Act, found at 50 U.S.C. §§ 501 et seq., as well as the Act's limitations.

The Soldiers' and Sailors' Civil Relief Act ("the Act") was passed to tackle the unique problems that servicepersons encounter trying to balance their personal financial lives and the rigors of military service. Specifically, the Act can provide a serviceperson temporary relief from evictions, lease terminations, installment sales contracts, repossessions, mortgage foreclosures on real and personal property, high interest rates, and suits against the serviceperson. But the Act does have limitations: once the serviceperson's military service no longer interferes with his ability to handle his personal obligations, the serviceperson is no longer protected by the Act.

Who Does the Act Protect?

The Soldiers' and Sailors' Civil Relief Act applies to all persons in "military service." This includes people in the Army, Navy, Air Force, Marine Corps, Coast Guard, and members of the Public Health Service who are on active duty. Reservists and members of the National Guard are protected when they are on active duty.

The Act covers those on "active duty," in training, and those getting education preliminary to induction into military service. Servicepersons who are absent from duty due to sickness are also covered by the Act.

In general, a military person's spouse and dependents are also covered under the Act, unless a Court decides that they can easily continue with their obligations whether or not the serviceperson (upon whom they are dependant) is in the military.

Which of Your Obligations Does the Act Cover?

The Act's protections do not cover all of a serviceperson's obligations. Before relying on the Act's protections, it is important to understand the limits to the Act's coverage:

1. The Act does not protect you from **criminal** proceedings. If you are arrested and tried, you cannot postpone the criminal case because you are in military service. The Act only covers a serviceperson's **civil** obligations.

2. The Act only **postpones** civil obligations; it does not permanently remove them. For example, if you default on a loan payment, you may be protected under the Act as long as your military service interferes with your ability to pay. However, once you are out of military service, or you get a raise and can easily pay your obligation, the Act may not protect you anymore.

3. For the most part, the Act only postpones a civil obligation if the serviceperson's ability to comply in full is **materially affected** by his or her military service. A court would look to a variety of factors to see if your ability to continue with your obligation is materially affected, such as:

   - your geographic and economic challenges;
   - the amount of your available leave;
   - your specific duty requirements; and
   - a comparison of your pre-service income to your military income.

   For example, if your relocation to Korea made it difficult or impossible for you to make monthly payments on your car loan, you may get temporary relief under the Act.

4. The Act only covers **written** agreements. Any oral agreement you have with a creditor will not be protected under the Act.

5. The Act only covers civil obligations under written agreement that servicepersons incurred **before** they entered military service. Any debts that military members incur during or after military service are not covered under the Act-the serviceperson would have to pay the debt back on the terms of the agreement. For instance, if you buy a car while you are in military service and later you can't make the car payments, you are not protected under the Act because you did not get the car loan before you entered military service.

If you meet all of the above requirements, the Act will provide you with the temporary relief necessary while your military service prevents you from managing your personal affairs. You would be protected from a creditor or collection agency collecting a debt by civil suit, from a judgement creditor's enforcement of that judgment by a lien on your property or wage garnishment, from foreclosure on property, from repossession, from eviction, and from termination of your lease. The Act also can reduce your interest rate on debts.

Even if the serviceperson is not the primary borrower under a contract, he or she may be protected by the Act. The Act protects persons in military service who are secondarily liable under a contract, which includes sureties, guarantors, endorsers, accommodation makers, or co-signers. For instance, let's say you co-signed a loan for your brother before you entered military service, and your brother stopped paying on the loan and filed bankruptcy. The lender now looks to you for payment. If you are still in military service and that service materially affects your ability to pay your brother's loan, you are temporarily protected under the Act.

If the serviceperson changes the terms of a contract in writing, during or after the time he is in military service, he would no longer be protected under the Act. The new contract with the new terms would govern. Accordingly, if you changed terms, terminated or cancelled the contract, or agreed to allow the lender to repossess or foreclose, you must follow those new terms.

How Does the Act Protect Me?

If you are a person in military service, you have a civil obligation that you incurred before you entered military service, and you are having a hard time making that obligation, you may get temporary relief in many situations. Outlined below are examples of exactly how and with what situations the Act can protect a person in military service.

Default Judgments

Normally, if you are a defendant in a civil lawsuit and you do not appear at a scheduled court hearing, the court would enter a "default judgment." The default judgment has the same effect as if you appeared in court, stated your defense, and lost. This is particularly troublesome for a person in the military who frequently relocates—it can be difficult for that person to appear at a court proceeding. Under the Act, before entering a default judgment, the plaintiff (the person suing you) must file an affidavit with the court swearing that the defendant (you) is not in military service. If the plaintiff does not file this affidavit, any default judgment is "voidable," or cancelable. If the plaintiff knows you are in military service but lies and says you aren't, he has committed a crime.

If a defendant is in military service and does not appear at the court proceeding, the court will appoint an attorney to represent the defendant and protect his interests. The attorney is responsible to get a "stay" of the court proceeding, (postpone the proceeding), and contact the serviceperson. Acts of the court-appointed attorney are not binding on the serviceperson, so if the attorney makes a mistake, the serviceperson may not be bound by that mistake.

If it ends up that a serviceperson gets a default judgment filed against him, he can void the default judgment and reopen the case by petitioning the court within 90 days after termination of military service. The petition must show that the serviceperson's ability to defend himself in court was "materially affected" by military service, and that he had a defense with merit. If the court decides that military service did not prejudice the serviceperson from making a defense, then the judgment stands. For instance, a soldier who remains in service for 20 years or has been assigned to one post for a long time may not have a hard time attending the proceeding and defending himself. If the court thinks this is true, the default judgment will stand.

Stay of Proceedings

When a serviceperson's military service prevents him from suing another party or from defending himself when sued, the Act permits a "stay" or postponement of the civil court proceedings. Once again, you would have to show that your military service has a material effect on your ability to prepare for and attend a court proceeding. The court may stay a court proceeding while the serviceperson is in military service or within 60 days thereafter. The stay can last as long as the person is in military service and for three months after he stops military service, but courts often grant shorter stays. Basically, the proceeding is postponed for as long as the serviceperson's military service prevents him from preparing for and attending court.

During the stay, the other party cannot penalize the serviceperson for not complying with any contract.

The court may stay any stage of a court proceeding, including postponing a judgment creditor's collection of a judgment. A court can remove or postpone a creditor's attachment or garnishment of a debtor's property, whether before or after judgment. For example, the court can delay a creditor from garnishing your wages to satisfy a judgment until your military service no longer interferes, or three months after military service, whichever is sooner.

If the person in military service is a co-defendant with others, the court may permit the plaintiff to proceed against the other defendants who are not in military service.

It is important for you to understand that the Act is not a permanent shield from any action of a creditor. The Act just allows the serviceperson to be represented by an attorney if the serviceperson is not present in court, and that attorney should stay the proceedings and let the serviceperson know about them. Once a serviceperson's military service no longer interferes with the serviceperson's ability to go to court, the proceedings continue.

Statute of Limitations

The "statute of limitations" is the amount of time that someone has to sue another person. For example, if you default on loan or credit card payments, your creditor has a certain number of years from the time you defaulted, decided under your state's laws, in which to sue you to collect the amount you owe. It can be difficult to sue someone who wronged you within the statute of limitations if you are in the military and you are on active duty, living abroad, or frequently relocating.

Under the Act, the time that you are in military service does not count in the running of any statute of limitations. This means that any potential suit by the serviceperson or against the serviceperson can be brought within the statute of limitations period plus the amount of time that the serviceperson was within military service. The extension of the statute of limitations applies to any proceeding in any court, board, bureau, commission, department, or other agency of government, no matter when the reason for the suit occurred. This extension does not apply to any limitation period prescribed by the IRS.

Under the Act, the extension of the statute of limitations should be automatic. In other words, it should not be a requirement that your military service materially affect your ability to bring or defend against suit. However, you should check your state laws. Some states have found that automatically extending the statute of limitations is unfair if a serviceperson's military service does not prevent him from filing or defending suit.

Housing

If a military member can't pay rent because of his or her military service, the Act may protect the member from eviction. You may be protected from being evicted if:

- The eviction is attempted during your military service;
- You, your spouse, children or other dependants occupy the premises for dwelling purposes;
- Your monthly rent does not exceed $1,200; and
- Your ability to pay is "materially affected" by your military service.

If all these requirements are met, the court may postpone eviction for up to three months.

Under the Act, new military members can also terminate a lease for a private dwelling if they entered the lease before beginning military service. Once the serviceperson enters active duty or receives orders, he can give the landlord written notice that he is terminating the lease because of military service. The effective date of the termination will depend upon the type of lease. For month-to-month rentals, it works like this: after a landlord receives your notice of lease termination, you will still owe the next rent payment, and your lease is terminated 30 days after that payment. For example, if your landlord receives your notice of termination on August 20, and your next payment is due on September 1, you would be responsible to pay the September 1 rent payment, and your termination will take effect on October 1.

The effective date of termination for all other leases is the last day of the month following the month you deliver the notice of termination. For example, if you give notice of termination on August 31, the lease will be terminated September 30.

Installment Contracts

An installment contract includes mortgages, car loans, other secured loans such as loans on large appliances or electrical goods, or lease-to-buy contracts. A service member who enters into an installment contract before entering active duty is protected under the Act if his ability to make payments is materially affected by military service. This means that if you have a hard time making payments under a contract because of your military service, you can get relief.

If you do not pay during your military service or for three months after you stop military service, your creditor can't cancel or terminate the contract, sell, foreclose, repossess, or seize your property unless (1) the court previously ordered the sale, foreclosure, or seizure, or (2) during or after military service you signed a new contract with new terms. However, it is important to understand that he may be able to seize the property if he goes to court first.

If a lender sues a serviceperson for not paying under a contract, and the serviceperson's ability to follow the contract is materially affected by his military service, the court may postpone the suit (see "Stay of Proceedings" above) or make "equitable disposition." If the court chooses to make equitable disposition, the court would have objective persons appraise any property under the contract. The court may then allow the creditor to foreclose on property, resume possession of property, or rescind (cancel) or terminate the contract, but only if the creditor pays the serviceperson an amount that the court decides is fair. The court could also require that the serviceperson pay all or part of prior installments or deposits as a condition of terminating the contract and keeping possession of property.

If a lender takes your property without a court order, he can be fined and/or imprisoned. For example, if you are unable to continue paying your car loan because you enter military service, your lender cannot repossess your car without going to court first. The court may postpone the repossession, allow repossession with some compensation to you, or allow you to keep the car after compensating the lender. If your lender repossesses your car, he can be fined or put in jail.

Interest Rates

You have the right to reduce the interest rate of any contract you entered before you entered military service to 6%, unless your military service does not materially affect your ability to pay the original (presumably higher) interest rate. This reduction includes service charges, renewal charges, fees or any other charges connected to the debt. The debtor must give the creditor written notice that he or she has entered active duty military service and request the reduction. Any creditor who wishes to return to the original, higher interest rate must petition the court and prove that entering active duty did not materially affect the debtor's ability to pay the original interest rate. Courts normally compare the debtor's pre-service income to his military income to determine whether or not his financial condition changed. If the debtor is making the same or more income while in active duty, the serviceperson will probably not get the reduction in interest rate. For example, if you are a "career soldier" and your military service does not prevent you from paying the full amount of your credit card interest, you will not be able to reduce the rate to 6%.

This reduction in the interest rate does not extend to the dependents or spouses of service members.

Insurance

Under the Act, a service member's private life insurance policy is protected against lapse, or forfeiture for nonpayment of premiums while the serviceperson is in military service and for one year thereafter. The insured or beneficiary must apply to the Veteran's Administration for protection under the Act. Also, any health insurance in effect the day before active military service started is automatically reinstated.

State Taxes

Servicepersons must pay state income taxes and personal property taxes for the state of their legal residence. Servicepersons who frequently relocate may wonder which state is considered their legal residence. The Act clarifies this for service members. A member does not lose legal residence solely because of a transfer pursuant to military orders. For example, if a member is a Virginia resident and is transferred to a base in California, the member will not lose Virginia residency nor be subject to California state income tax on military pay.

For state personal property taxes, the Act exempts a nonresident who is relocated to a state from personal property taxes in that state, if the personal property is titled solely in the name of the service person. If you have joint property with a nonmilitary member, the property is taxable to the jurisdiction where it is located.

Adverse Actions

Creditors and insurers are prohibited from taking adverse actions against service members who exercise their rights under the Act. This means:

- A prospective lender cannot determine that a serviceperson cannot pay because he took advantage of the Act.

- A current creditor cannot change terms to an existing arrangement, or put a mark on the serviceperson's credit report because the service person takes advantage of the Act.

- An insurer cannot refuse to insure because the serviceperson invoked the Act.

The Soldiers' and Sailors' Civil Relief Act was enacted to help servicepersons whose military service hinders their ability to manage their daily finances. In other words, the Act is meant for a serviceperson who is reassigned to another post or overseas and/or whose income drops significantly. The Act's protections should not be used to lower interest rates, avoid suit, or stop paying debts if the serviceperson's military service does not materially impair his ability to do these things. If it appears that a service person is abusing the Act, the court may enforce civil liabilities without regard to the protective provisions of the Act.

CHAPTER 29

How to Cut Your Holiday Bills in Half Without Feeling Like a Scrooge

If you usually find yourself in January and February facing a stack of bills from holiday shopping, resolve that this year, you aren't going to let the spending get out of hand. Decide that your holiday memories are going to be happy ones, not headaches! Following are strategies for spending less while enjoying your holidays a lot more.

Credit Strategies

The perfect, fun-filled, gift-laden holiday season is just a matter of buying the right holiday trappings, right? That's certainly what advertisers want you to believe. But you don't have to fall into the trap of charging your way through the holidays, or you'll find yourself paying for it for a long, long time. Be smart about how you use credit, and stay in control:

- Avoid "buy now and pay later" offers designed to encourage you to spend money you don't have. These plans usually charge high interest from the date of purchase if you can't pay off the bill in full by the end of the no-interest period, or if you are just one day late with a payment. If you can't afford to pay for it now, you can't afford to buy it now.

- Consider carrying only two credit cards for shopping. Use one (with a zero balance) for purchases you will pay off in full. Use the other (a low-interest-rate card) for purchases you'll pay off over time, but quickly! If you are already carrying credit card balances from last year, leave all your cards at home to avoid temptation.

"I'm glad that's done. Now all we have to do is wrap the presents, write the holiday cards, cook dinner, and somehow manage to get out of debt!"

- Keep track of your holiday purchases. Most people carry eight to ten pieces of plastic, so it's easy to lose track of holiday credit card purchases, then be in for a big shock when the bills arrive. Record *all* holiday purchases in your checkbook register or use Debt Counselors of America's On-Track[sm] program (www.GetOutOfDebt.org) to monitor where the money's going.

- Use a low rate bank card instead of high-rate department store cards unless you are absolutely certain you can pay the bill in full. The savings can be dramatic. For example, if you have a $1,000 balance on a card that charges 19.8% and you just make the minimum payment over time, it will cost almost $845 in interest and take more than eight years to pay off. But if your interest rate is 14%, your interest charges will be closer to $450, and it will take about six years and eight months to pay off.

- Avoid "skip a payment" offers that are as common as Santa around the holidays. You'll just pay more interest and face a larger bill the next month.

Gifts

Be honest: can you even remember what gifts you received or gave over the past couple of years? We often give pricey gifts because we feel guilty or pressured. Then to top it off, we also feel broke! It truly can be "the thought that counts" if you're thoughtful in your gift-giving. Make your list and check it twice. Do you *really* need to give all those gifts?

- For younger kids, consider giving only one or two larger gifts instead of overwhelming them with a pile of smaller gifts—especially if they can expect gifts from relatives or friends.

- For older kids, have them decide what they really want, then consider gift certificates which will allow them to buy what they want right after Christmas, when holiday sales offer lower prices. They can pocket the difference, or buy even more for the same amount of money.

- For family members, discuss drawing names so you only have to buy one gift instead of many. Or, agree upon a spending limit per person. Enlarged and framed family photographs make terrific holiday gifts for parents and grandparents who have "everything." Help kids make personal homemade gifts for their relatives. Even videotapes or tape recordings can be more fun than many store-bought gifts.

- Consider homemade gifts of food, plants, or even services, for family members, teachers or co-workers.

- For all gifts, shop as early as possible for the best selection and prices. You won't get stuck paying a fortune for some gift you aren't sure is even right.

- Online shopping can make your season less stressful. Make sure you understand refund policies, and don't forget to include shipping charges in your budget.
- Make inexpensive wrapping paper by stamping brown packaging paper with festive ink or paint stamps.
- Send holiday post cards instead of cards, and save on postage. If you're too busy to send cards before the holidays, consider sending New Year's cards in early January.
- Teach kids the value of giving. Have them donate used toys and clothing to charity. You may also be able to take a tax deduction.

Entertaining

You don't have to try to outdo Martha Stewart when it comes to holiday entertaining! Do what you enjoy, and skip the rest. You'll be a lot happier and so will your family. To save time and money:

- Organize a cookie exchange. Each person bakes a large batch of one kind of cookie, then exchanges cookies with others.
- Buy baking and cooking ingredients in bulk when they're on sale. Freeze extras or split them with a friend.
- Keep everyday meals simple so you'll have time to enjoy other activities. Make a list of five or six simple dishes your family will eat, and rotate them over and over again throughout the month.
- Focus on activities besides shopping. Read holiday stories with younger children, and start holiday traditions with kids of any age. It's likely your kids will enjoy and remember those experiences long after the gifts have been forgotten.
- When you throw a party, make it potluck. Pick a theme, provide the main dish and perhaps beverages, then let your guests bring a dish to pass around. (They'll probably feel obligated to bring something anyway.)
- Consider traveling before or after the holidays. You can save a lot of money on airfares and avoid long waits or heavy traffic as well.

CHAPTER 30

How to Send Your Kids Back to School Without Breaking the Bank

As ready as you may be to see your kids back in school after summer break, you may well be dreading back-to-school shopping, and the drain it will place on your wallet. With some careful shopping and smart planning, though, you may be able to stick to your budget and get the kids what they need.

There's one strategy that will make your job a lot easier: plan early. Talk with each child and create a back-to-school plan before the end of summer break rolls around. Planning will give you time to shop for bargains, and give your children time to earn some money if you can't or won't get them everything they want.

Most kids can understand basic budgeting concepts, which you can adjust depending on their ages. Younger children can help you make a list of what they might need, and will benefit by talking with you about the differences between needs and wants. Older children will especially benefit by learning how to create their own budgets, negotiating with you what you will cover, and then finding a way to either earn more money, or make choices about what they really want.

Following are some specific suggestions for sending your children back to school without breaking the bank.

Supplies

- Create your shopping list as early as possible to allow for bargain shopping throughout the summer.

- Visit dollar stores for inexpensive supplies, such as off-brand inexpensive tape, glue, etc. Discount office supply stores can also be a good place to buy supplies.

- Back-to-school sales can offer some of the best prices of the year. Shop when they begin for the best selection.

- Throughout the year, keep an eye on office supply store clearance bins and sales. Stock up when prices are low, and save supplies for later.

- Kids can get into recycling. Urge them to use supplies left from the previous year.

- Small children will enjoy "dressing up" plain notebooks, pencils, or even lunch boxes with pictures or stickers. This will also give them something to do when they complain of boredom on a rainy summer day.

- Organize a sale on school supplies at your children's school. Negotiate a deal with a local office supply store or discount office supply store and everyone can save.

- Check out office supply catalogs such as Quill (1-800-789-1331; www.quillcorp.com) and Reliable (1-800-735-4000; www.reliable.com). You may want to join with other parents to negotiate a group discount.

- Consider quality when buying items that can last more than one year, such as backpacks. Alternatively, keep an eye out at garage sales for used items. (It's easier to pass secondhand items on to younger children than older ones, but it can always be worth a try.)

- Don't forget to find out exactly what your child will need for school, and be aware of any rules regarding certain types of supplies that might or might not be allowed.

- Businesses will sometimes give away leftover supplies such as preprinted conference binders, note pads, or pens. Hold a drive with local businesses and request donations.

- Consider upgraded or refurbished computers if your child needs one. Canvass local businesses for donations of computers that are outdated but can be upgraded.

Clothing

- Organize a friend/neighbor/relative swap. Get together and trade clothes that your children have outgrown. Again, this works best with younger children, but if your older children know they have a certain budget to stick to, they may be open to creative ideas.

- Shop early in the summer for end-of-season clothes kids can wear in the fall. At the end of summer, shop for items your kids can wear next spring.

- Try garage sales and thrift shops. Bargains are out there!

- With your older children, establish a budget. Then give them some leeway to choose what they want to buy—within your guidelines. If they want expensive name-brand items, they'll learn they may have to give up something else.

- Keep your eye open throughout the year for basics that are on sale for good prices. When you see a good sale, take advantage of it. If you do buy end-of-season clothes, consider buying them in a larger size so your kids will grow into them the next year.

- Buy your kids some new clothes for school, but insist they wear older ones when they are hanging around at home or playing outdoors.

Food

- Avoid small packaged convenience foods for lunch boxes. Instead, buy snacks like chips or cookies in bulk and repackage them into individual plastic bags yourself. (The kids can help!) Recycle those plastic bags for even more savings.

- Make muffins in large batches and freeze them for a quick and healthy breakfast or lunchbox item.

- Make tortilla roll up sandwiches. You can make several days worth and refrigerate or freeze them for the week. This is another project where the kids can help.

- Plan a week's worth of school lunches on the weekend and enlist your children's help in making sure you have the ingredients. Prepackage whatever you can to save time, hassles and money.

Activities

- With your kids, decide on a spending budget for activities like sports, clubs or special events. Then let them raise any money they need over the limit.

- If other kid's birthday parties are costing you a fortune, talk with other parents about holding parties without gifts, or pooling funds for one larger gift. If that doesn't work, give your kids a "gift allowance" and let them make up the difference if they go over the budget. Younger kids typically receive more gifts than they can enjoy at one time anyway.

- Consider buying children's toys, candy, and snacks in bulk when they go on sale: you'll save money and won't have to scramble to buy or make something when your child remembers an upcoming school event or birthday party at the last minute.

CHAPTER 31

How to Use Credit Cards in College and Not Get in Over Your Head

Let's face it: when it comes to getting credit, most students have it easy these days. Most college students do get credit cards—and plenty of them if they want. According to a recent study for the Education Resources Institute and the Institute for Higher Education Policy, two-thirds of college students have credit cards, and a quarter of them got their first card as a high school student.

The good news is that most college students are pretty careful with their cards and don't run up huge balances they can't pay back. But at Debt Counselors of America, we've heard from enough students (and parents) to know that some do. When that does happen, it can create a lot of problems. So it's worth the time to help students learn how to use those tempting pieces of plastic carefully, and avoid a hefty tab by graduation.

The advantages of credit cards are the same for students as anyone else: they're convenient, you can "buy now, pay later," and they can help you build an excellent credit rating. After all, the best reference you'll find on a credit report is a major credit card paid on time, all the time. A good credit rating can be a big plus when you graduate and start looking for a job, place to live, and perhaps even a car loan.

The main disadvantage to credit cards is that they don't always feel like "real money," so it's easy to charge more than you can really afford. You can easily wind up with big balances that will be a huge drain on your finances once you're out of school. And don't assume you'll be able to easily handle those bills when you get your first job. Most graduates are surprised at how far their first paycheck *doesn't* go. The less debt you have to worry about, the better.

What is the best way, then, for a student to use credit cards?

Don't feel you have to take every offer that comes along. Sure, that free T-shirt they give you just for signing up would be nice. But it won't seem like such a bargain if you're paying off that card for the next ten years. You're better off sticking with one major card, maybe two if you really need it. There will be less temptation and fewer hassles, but at the same time, one or two cards paid on time will be a big boost for your credit rating.

Remember, it's not free! When you do get a card, repeat this phrase, "This is simply a way to access a loan. It is not free money." You can pay it back sooner (when you get the bill) or later (over time). If you pay over time, you'll be charged interest. That interest adds to the cost of the loan, and can really add up. If you just make the minimum payment, for example, you'll probably find that most of your payment goes to the lender, in the form of interest, not to pay off what you charged. Don't believe it? Look at your statement and see.

The Table below shows an example of how much it will cost you (in interest alone) and how long it will take you to pay back your balance at different interest rates if you just pay the minimum payment each month:

BALANCE	INTEREST RATE		
	14%	17%	19.8%
$500	$137/3 yrs. 7 mos.	$182/ 3 yrs 10 mos.	$232/4 yrs. 1 mo.
$1000	$455/6 yrs. 8 mos.	$629/ 7 yrs 5 mos.	$843/8 yrs. 4 mos.
$1500	$1728/11 yrs. 8 mos.	$2418/ 13 yrs 2 mos.	$$3278/15 yrs. 1 mo.

Source: *The Ultimate Credit Handbook* by DCA Education Advisor Gerri Detweiler

Always, always pay your credit card bills on time. Sounds obvious, but when cash is tight (which it usually is when you're in school), you may be tempted to let the bills slide for a little while then make a large payment to "make up for it"—maybe when that student loan check comes through. It's not a good idea. Not only will many lenders charge late fees if those payments aren't there on time, but any late payments will be reported to the credit bureaus and stay on your credit report for seven years, *even if you later pay the bill in full*. If you can't afford to make your minimum payments, a nonprofit credit and financial counseling agency like Debt Counselors of America (www.GetOutOfDebt.org) may be able to help. The worst thing you can do is wait, hoping the problem gets better while it only continues to get worse.

Check your credit report before you graduate. Your credit report is going to be just as important to your financial future as that diploma will be to job-hunting. It can be reviewed by lenders, insurance companies and even employers! Get a copy of yours before you graduate to make sure everything is correct and up-to-date. If you find mistakes, fill out the form enclosed with your report to notify the credit bureau so it can investigate. You can get your report from any of the following three major credit bureaus. It generally costs about $8.

Equifax: 1-800-685-1111, www.equifax.com

Experian: 1-888-397-3742, www.experian.com

TransUnion: 1-800-888-4213, www.transunion.com

Advice for Mom and Dad:

Like it or not, your children are going to get offers for lots of credit cards. You'd probably be amazed at how easy it is for them to get credit (even when you're their major source of income). You can handle this one of three ways:

- Ignore it, hope they don't get into too much trouble, and if they do, deal with it then. The problem with this approach is obvious: you may one day get that dreaded phone call saying the debt is out of control.

- Give your student a card before they leave for school, either by co-signing or having them added to one of your accounts. If you have the bills sent to you, instead of them, at least you'll know what's going on. The problem with this approach is twofold: first, if your offspring does go wild with the plastic, you might end up having to foot the bill or pay the consequences (late charges, marks on *your* credit file); and secondly, if you co-sign and the bills go to your child at school, you may not even find out that the payments aren't being made until it is much too late.

- Discuss credit cards with your kids well before they head off to school and then let them make their own decisions. Go over your bills with them so they can see how much those casual purchases add up, and how interest does too. Tell them about a time when money was tight and how you handled it. Decide together how many credit cards they should get and how they will use them. This option may be your best bet for keeping them out of trouble, and protecting your credit rating, too. Remember, if your student gets a card on his or her own, without you signing it, you won't be legally responsible for the bills. (But you may feel responsible anyway!)

How did you learn how to use credit cards? The hard way—through experience—right? Maybe your kids don't have to learn the same way. It may not seem like your teenagers are listening when you try to talk with them about credit, but chances are they'll remember what you said. Time spent helping them understanding the financial choices they'll soon face will be time well spent.

CHAPTER 32

How to Be Financially Successful When You Graduate

Congratulations! You've made it through the starving student years and now you're ready to start a job and earn some real money. You're probably thinking about all the things you'll be able to buy, places you'll go, and things you'll be able to do when those paychecks start rolling in.

Not so fast. If you're like lots of people and just assume you'll figure things out as you go along, you'll probably end up like a lot of people: in debt. But if you're smart about your money, you'll end up way ahead of the game.

Plan Ahead, Double Your Money

OK, we admit it. For most of us (except maybe some of the business majors) planning sounds boring, boring, boring. But what if we told you just a few hours with a paper and pencil might help you *double* your savings and investments? Research by Consumer Federation of America and NationsBank found that people with incomes as little as $10,000 to as much as $100,000 who reported having a written financial plan, also had *twice* as much money in savings and investments as people who said they didn't have a plan. Now does it sound a little more interesting?

You're probably not ready to hire a financial planner yet, but you can take a few hours to think about your goals—what you want, how much you need and how you plan to get there. Write down what you want, figure out how much it will cost and then look at how you can get the cash to get it. You probably have a lot of goals right now, like buying a car and vacationing in the Caribbean, but it's unlikely you'll be able to get it all right now. Be honest. If you can't swing as much as you'd like right now, scale back a little. Just put away what you can, and don't get into the trap of thinking that if you can't afford something, you can just borrow to get it. Otherwise, you'll wind up with a big chunk of that paycheck going to lenders every month.

A good exercise is to take one month to track every expenditure you have—every soda from a vending machine, coffee, snack, lunch out, pack of gum, etc. that you buy. After you spend a month doing this, you will be able to see areas where you can cut back on spending—drink coffee at home rather than buying it at work, bring a soda from home, and pack a lunch regularly. Make going out to lunch a treat rather than the norm. At the end of this chapter, we have included a list of "Money Gobblers" expenses that take a chunk out of many people's paychecks without their realizing it.

Where Does the Money Go?

Your salary may seem like a lot of money at first, but wait until you see how far it goes—or doesn't go! Along with the new feeling of having a regular income will be the experience of paying expenses that you've never had before. Before you even get your hands on your earnings, Uncle Sam and the other tax guys are going to take a nice chunk out of those checks. Then you'll have all kinds of living expenses, not to mention the things you just want. One study by the student financing organization, Sallie Mae, found that the average college grad needed to earn $38,512 before taxes just to support their graduation debts and financial obligations. Ouch!

So the first thing is to hold off on big purchases until you get a realistic picture of how much you need to cover your bills and have spending money. There may be some expenses you'll overlook until you actually start working (clothes for work, travel, food, subscriptions). You may be surprised at how fast your money goes, especially if you were living in a dorm and eating through a dining plan at a college cafeteria. Housing, utilities, and food cost a lot. The U.S. Department of Agriculture states that a man or woman between the ages of twenty and fifty should spend around $120 a month on food, so try to get a few months under your belt before you start spending.

Generally, before making any big changes in your financial picture, you should have enough money saved to be able to live for three to six months without an income. This is a good amount to cover any unexpected emergencies, layoffs, or if you decide this job just isn't for you.

Getting Around Without Going Broke

You gotta have a new set of wheels, right? And, the car dealer will probably tell you that you can get into a great car with really low monthly payments. But, wait a minute. More wheels will cost you a lot more than you probably realize. In fact, the average car will cost you nearly half a million dollars over your driving lifetime!

How is that possible? Well, cars cost a lot more than the payments. There's insurance, gas and maintenance, and they all add up. Before you let a new vehicle drive you to the poorhouse, think about your alternatives:

- **Buy a good used car.** A good used car that holds its value could be your best bet. That way, if things don't work out at your current job, you'll be able to sell it for at least as much as you owe. And, of course, it will cost less over the long run!

- **Forget a car and use public transportation.** If you really need to use a car for out-of-town trips or special occasions, consider renting one. It will be cheaper than owning one for a year!

Whatever you do, avoid buying or leasing a car that will obligate you to big monthly payments. What happens if you don't like your new job or it doesn't work out? How will you make the payments then? Also, steer clear of four and five-year car loans. If you need to sell the car after a couple of years, you'll probably find that you are "upside down" (owing more on the loan than the car is worth).

Paying for That Education

The six-month grace period on your student loans may give you some breathing room, but those six months fly by. Find out what your payments will be and figure them into your spending plan. Also consider paying extra each month to pay them off faster. You can always send in a few extra dollars with your payments, and over the long run, they will really add up!

Different lenders have different options to pay off student loans, but if you have a federal loan, you generally have the following repayment options:

1. **Standard Repayment Plan.** You make fixed monthly payments of at least $50 over a fixed period of time—up to ten years. Under this plan, you would probably pay the lowest total interest because the repayment period is shorter than that of the other plans.

2. **Extended Repayment Plan.** This plan gives you more leeway by extending repayment over a period of twelve to thirty years, depending on the total amount borrowed. You would still pay a fixed amount each month of at least $50, but monthly payments are probably less than under the Standard Repayment Plan. Remember, however, that you will probably pay more interest because the repayment period is longer.

3. **Graduated Repayment Plan.** Under this plan, your payments start small and increase every two years. This gives leeway to recent graduates whose incomes start low but increase steadily. The repayment period lasts twelve to thirty years

depending on the total amount borrowed. Again, if you use this repayment plan, you will probably pay more interest because the repayment period is longer.

4. **Income Contingent Repayment Plan.** This plan bases monthly payments on your income and the total amount of federal loans that you borrowed. Your monthly payments adjust with your income—the lower your income, the lower the payment, and vice versa. You would have up to twenty-five years to repay your student loans. After twenty-five years, any unpaid amount would be discharged but you will have to pay taxes on the discharged amount.

If you run into trouble and can't make your student loan payments, you may have several options until you're back on your feet. If you have a federal loan, you may be eligible for a **deferment** or **forbearance**. These options are only available to you if you talk with your lender before you fall behind on your payments, though, so you have to ask before you're too strapped. (See Chapter 3, "Drowning in Student Loans.")

A **deferment** allows you to postpone making payments on your loan (and even cancel certain federal loans) if you meet specific eligibility requirements. Some of the requirements for deferment or cancellation are:

- Economic hardship.
- You work as a full-time elementary or secondary school teacher in a designated area serving low-income students, you teach children with disabilities, or you teach math, science, foreign languages, bilingual education or other fields designated as teacher-shortage areas. (The Department of Education annually publishes the *Directory of Designated Low-Income Schools for Teacher Cancellation Benefits*. Check your school's financial aid office for this Directory.)
- You are a student in school.
- You are a parent or working mother.
- You are a full-time professional provider of early intervention services for the disabled or a full-time employee of a public or non-profit agency providing services to low-income, high-risk children and their families.
- You have a temporary total disability.
- You are unemployed.

Depending on the type of federal loan you have, the federal government may or may not pay the interest accruing during the deferment period. If you must pay the interest, you can do so by making interest-only payments during the deferment period or you can let the interest accumulate and be added to the loan amount when the deferment period ends.

Even if you have other unanticipated personal or health problems, but don't meet the requirements for a deferment, you may be able to get a **forbearance** of loan payments. During a forbearance period, you may make no payments or reduced payments. Interest will continue to accrue during the forbearance period and will be added to the loan amount when the forbearance period ends.

Home Sweet Home

Tired of dorm living or a crowded group house? Ready for that dream apartment, or maybe even a house? Before you sign a lease on a new place or even start house hunting, take some time to choose the best digs for your dollars. The general rule is that you should not pay more than 30% of your net monthly income on housing. If you are having a problem affording a lease, you can look for a landlord who will give you a break on the rent in exchange for some work on the place by you. Whatever route you take—living alone or with roommates—try to avoid long-term lease commitments until you are sure your job and any roommates will work out.

If you want to live on your own, look at all the expenses in the picture. Do you get free parking? Are utilities included in your monthly rent? If utilities are not included, your housing expenses will increase substantially. You may have bills for power, gas, telephone, water, and if you get cable, you add another $30 or so to your expenses each month. Also, if utilities are not included, you need to pay attention to things that will jack up your power bill. Take into account such considerations as whether or not you're in an older home, whether you have an air conditioning unit, and whether or not you have central heat.

If you go the roommate route, you need to be careful to protect yourself. There are plenty of horror stories out there about people who weren't careful and end up with huge financial responsibilities. Make sure that all roommates are on the lease, so that all roommates are equally responsible for the lease payments. Make sure you are confident that your roommates can afford their share of the lease payment. Keep in mind that each person listed on the lease will be liable for the full lease payment if another person on the lease doesn't pay his or her share.

A lot of people mistakenly think that they don't have to worry about their roommate's irresponsible behavior. You could end up losing your deposit if your roommates damage the property or skip out on the lease. You may believe that you aren't responsible for your roommate's irresponsible financial behavior, but any late or non-payment of rent caused by your roommate can affect you for a long time. Even if your late rent payments don't show up on your credit report (and stay there for the seven-year reporting period), they will hurt you when you are ready to move into a new apartment or house.

You should use the same caution with your utilities. If you get utilities in your name, you are responsible for all payments due, and it is up to you to get reimbursed by your roommates. If you try to hold out and wait until your roommates are ready to pay their share, and the utility bill payment is late, this late payment can be reflected on your credit report and hurt you later in life, even though it wasn't really "your fault."

To protect yourself and make sure your bills are paid on time, you should come up with a system with your roommates. Some roommates put different utilities in different roommates' names, so that no one person is personally responsible for all utility bills. The roommate in charge of a particular bill can divide the bill amount by the number of roommates, and require each roommate to pay his or her share 10 days before the actual due date to make sure the bill payment is sent on time. You can have "bill night" where all roommates get together, order pizza, and pay the bills. Another way to make sure all roommates are protected is to have each roommate put a certain amount of money in an account—totaling $500 or so, to cover unexpected emergencies.

A great (although usually unattainable) option for college grads with the time, energy and money is to buy a house that needs some work and fix it up. If you decide to buy a house, make sure you can put down 20% on a down payment. Although low down payment loans are available, if you decide to move in the next few years, you could wind up owning more than your house is worth. A larger down payment can keep you out of that trap. If you can rent part of it to roommates, you may end up with a great low-cost investment on your hands.

Plastic Pointers

Those credit cards may seem like your passport to the good life right now. But nothing will sink you faster than an overloaded wallet that's always getting a workout.

Here's the reality: credit cards are great for convenience and to help you out in a jam, but if you run up a lot of bills you can't pay quickly, you'll pay a hefty price for that convenience. Refer to the chart in Chapter 31 which shows how much you'll pay in interest and how long it will take you to pay off a balance if you only make the minimum payment on your credit cards.

It's a pretty good bet that two major credit cards will be enough. You can use one for day-to-day purchases that you pay in full. The other card should have the lowest interest rate you can find, and you'll save that one for real emergencies when you know you won't be able to pay it in full.

If you don't have a major credit card when you graduate, it'll be tough to get that first one. This is truly a case where you'll find out that it takes credit to get credit. If you find yourself in that bind, consider a secured credit card, which is a major credit card that requires a security deposit. Pay your bills on time each month and it shouldn't take long to build a good credit rating and get all the credit you want.

Protect Your Credit Record

A lot of recent graduates make the mistake of charging up now with the expectation that they'll be able to pay it all off later, when they are making the big bucks. They believe that they'll get a high paying job soon enough, and at that time, they'll have no problem paying off all their debt in full. That may or may not be true, but regardless, those months or years of nonpayment will be on their credit report for seven years.

Your credit report is your key to your good financial future. Anytime you need credit—for a mortgage, an auto loan, a credit card, student loans for graduate school, even getting a lease on an apartment—your creditor will look at your credit report to determine if you are a good credit risk. Some recent graduates who don't pay attention to their credit reports now will get a big surprise later when they want to buy a new car and can only get an auto loan with a 20% interest rate.

Negative information stays on your credit report for seven years, and can stay on your report for life if you apply for a loan or insurance for more than $150,000, or if you get a job that pays at least a $75,000 salary. You keep your credit report clean by consistently paying your bills on time, and having a reasonable amount of debt and open credit. The more consistent your payment history in your credit report, the better credit risk you are. You may also refer to Chapters 7, 8, 10, and 12 to learn more about credit reports.

It's a good idea to get a copy of your credit report to see what information it has. There may be inaccurate information in the report that you should dispute. A dispute form should accompany the credit report, and you should include a copy of any documentation that you have that shows the information is wrong.

Get Ahead Now

Now's the time to start saving and investing for your future. "But I have no money!" you complain. Come on! Do you really think it's going to be easier "someday?" The more you make, the more you'll want to spend. So get in the habit of saving now. Starting early means you'll have to put aside a lot less to reach your goals than if you wait.

Here's an example from *The Truth About Money*, a great money book by Ric Edelman. Suppose you've set a goal of having $100,000 socked away by retirement at age 65. (You'll need a lot more than that, but this is just an illustration.) If you start saving at age 20, assuming a 10% return, you'll need to put aside only $9 a month. If you wait until you're 30, you'll have to invest $26 a month; at age forty it becomes $75 a month; and if you really procrastinate, at age 50 you'll have to sock away $239 a month. Starting early pays off big time!

If you're intimidated by investments, consider starting an investment club or joining one in your area. Generally, there are a lot of tools that you can use to save including money market funds, investing in stocks, traditional and Roth IRAs, or simple savings accounts. One of the easiest ways to save is to have money taken directly out of your paycheck. An example of this is a 401(k) plan through your employer. A 401(k) plan is a great way to save, especially if your employer matches your contributions.

Matching works as follows: if you put 10% of your gross monthly paycheck (before taxes) into a 401(k) account, your employer would put in a matching amount into your account. After a certain vesting period (during which time you must continue working for that employer—maybe 2-5 years) the matching amount is guaranteed. If your employer offers a 401(k) plan, find out (1) how much your employer matches (some employers don't match at all), (2) what the total amount that you can contribute to the 401(k) plan is, (3) how long you must work before you can start contributing to your 401(k) plan, and (4) how long the vesting period is. If your employer does match, a 401(k) is one of the best saving tools you have for retirement—no other investment has a 100% return on your investment.

Whatever investment tool you choose, start saving something *now*. That means today!

When the Going Gets Tough

Not everything will be smooth sailing from here on out. You can't predict what may happen; the economy could go south for a while, you could become ill and have to leave work, or your job may not be there. If you've kept yourself out of too much debt and saved part of every paycheck, you'll weather the storms a lot easier. But if you do get into a rough spot, Debt Counselors of America® is there to help.

Good luck!

Money Gobblers

Here is a list of potential money gobblers-things which are likely to eat at your cash flow. There is no intent to categorize these as good or bad, approved or disapproved. It just helps remind us of all those little expenses.

Aerobics .... _____	Car Washes .... _____
Anniversary .... _____	Cassette Tapes .... _____
Antiques .... _____	CD Club .... _____
Arts & Crafts .... _____	Child Support .... _____
Auto Club .... _____	Child's Transport .... _____
Baby Pictures .... _____	Christmas Gifts .... _____
Baby Sitting .... _____	Cigarettes .... _____
Bank Charges .... _____	Classes .... _____
Batteries .... _____	Club Dues .... _____
Beauty Parlor/Barber .... _____	Coffee Expense .... _____
Beauty Supplies .... _____	Computer Disks/Supplies ...... _____
Beverages .... _____	Cruising .... _____
Bike/ Bike Access .... _____	Dating Services .... _____
Bingo .... _____	Diaper Service .... _____
Birth Control .... _____	Dietary Service .... _____
Birthdays .... _____	Dinners Out .... _____
Boat/Boat Supplies .... _____	Domestic Help .... _____
Books .... _____	Door-to-Door Salesmen .... _____
Bottled Water .... _____	Contact Lenses .... _____
Bounced Checks .... _____	Education Supplies .... _____
Bus Passes .... _____	Encyclopedias .... _____
Cable/Premium Channels ...... _____	Entertainment .... _____
Car Pool .... _____	Fast Food Attack .... _____
Car Rental .... _____	Father's/Mother's Day .... _____

Fishing	_____	Photo Supplies/Film	_____
Fun Runs/10K	_____	Plants	_____
Garden Supplies	_____	Postage	_____
Greeting Cards	_____	Races	_____
Guns	_____	Road/Bridge Tolls	_____
Gym/Weight Room	_____	School Tuition/Lunches	_____
Hobbies	_____	Sick Leave	_____
Household Items	_____	Skating	_____
Internet Access	_____	Slots	_____
Lessons	_____	Small Appliances	_____
Liquor/Alcohol	_____	Sports/Sporting Events	_____
Lottery	_____	Stamps	_____
Lunches	_____	Stationary	_____
Phone Cards	_____	Stereo	_____
Magazines	_____	Summer Camp	_____
Mail Orders	_____	Taxicabs	_____
Make-Up	_____	Tobacco	_____
Medications	_____	Toilet Articles	_____
Multi-Level Marketing	_____	Trash Pick Up	_____
Munchies	_____	Tupperware	_____
Motor Bike Expenses	_____	TV Rental	_____
Movies	_____	TV Shopping	_____
Music Lessons	_____	Vacation	_____
Night Out	_____	Valentines Day	_____
Pantyhose	_____	Video Games	_____
Paper Products	_____	Video Rentals	_____
Parking/Speeding tickets	_____		
Pet Supplies	_____	**Total**	_____

CHAPTER 33

How to Come Back From Vacation With Money in Your Pocket

Sometimes you just need to get away from it all. But vacations can be expensive, and the last thing you'll want is to come home to a stack of bills from your too few days of fun. In this chapter we'll give you tips for making your next vacation affordable, less stressful, and even more enjoyable. And who knows? You might even come back with money in your pocket!

What's Your Plan?

Budgeting may not be the most fun part of vacation planning, but it's essential.

According to the American Automobile Association, a family of four should budget at least $225 per day for transportation, lodging and meals. Here's the breakdown: $100 a day for meals, $110 a day for lodging, and about $11-$15 per 100 miles of traveling for automobile costs. That, of course, applies to vacations where you'll be driving to your destination. If you plan to travel overseas or far from home, you'll have to budget for airfare and local transportation.

It sounds obvious, but your vacation dollars will go much further if you have a plan and allow yourself plenty of time to find the best deals. If your usual scenario is to decide you just "have" to go somewhere, scrape up what cash you can, then put the rest on plastic, your vacation is likely to cost you *a lot* more than if you had planned ahead.

There's no reason you can't start planning for next year's vacation now. Sit down with your family or traveling companions and start brainstorming destinations, types of activities, when you want to go, how many places you want to visit, etc. Then visit a travel agent, your local library, or check out some Internet-based travel sites to get an idea of how much your fantasy trip will cost.

Once you have an idea of what you want, decide how much you can realistically afford and start to shape your vacation around that budget. Set a weekly or bi-weekly savings goal and get the whole family involved. One family wanted to go to Disney World for years, but never had the money. Debt Counselors of America (www.GetOutOfDebt.org) showed them how to create a budget, then Mom drew a thermometer-style chart to hang in the kitchen so the family can keep track of their vacation savings. Next year, they'll be shaking hands with Mickey!

Hold a garage sale or find another way to raise your seed money. Ask everyone in the family to come up with creative ways to save money toward the vacation. You may be surprised at what your kids can do when they are motivated! All special earnings or savings should be put in the vacation fund, off-limits to the family. You may want to buy a piggy bank that can't be opened until its broken if someone in the family might be tempted to dip into the fund.

Your goal should be to have enough cash saved to cover your budget for your trip. Creating a plan for your trip is the best way to prepare.

Cutting Costs

Here are some more travel tips to make that vacation affordable:

Travel off-season whenever possible. Visiting a popular location just a week or two before or after the busy season can mean substantially lower costs, fewer crowds and proprietors bending over backwards to make sure you enjoy your stay. If you have a certain vacation time in mind (August, for example) look for locations where August is considered off-season, rather than following the crowds.

Driving there...

When traveling by car, pack snacks, treats, sodas or juices, and staples like peanut butter and jelly sandwich ingredients or cereal for the kids. You'll easily save money and face fewer arguments with the kids at each fuel stop.

Make sure your kids have enough money to enjoy the trip without asking you for cash every time you turn around. Ahead of time, set guidelines describing what you'll pay for and what you expect them to cover. ("We'll buy your meals, but you'll be expected to buy any other food, like snacks." Or, "we'll give you $35 to spend at the amusement park, but the rest is up to you.") Then help them find ways to raise spending money, by doing chores for you or neighbors, holding a bake sale, etc.

Before you take your car on the road, get an oil change, properly inflate the tires and make sure there aren't any mechanical troubles waiting to happen. The last thing you want is to spend a fortune on repairs with a mechanic you don't know.

Flying there...

You should call at least three airlines, or use a good travel agent, to compare prices. The sooner you start shopping, the better. Consider smaller, no-frills airlines as well as airports that are less popular. Fares at Chicago's Midway airport, for example, can be much cheaper than those to and from O'Hare. Similarly, smaller airlines like Southwest often offer attractive deals. Typically, you'll get the best fares on Tuesday, Wednesday and Saturday, and if you stay over a Saturday night. Holiday times can be very expensive, so avoid peak days. (See our list of Internet-travel sites where you can check for low fares.)

You may be able to get a cheap fare through a consolidator or discount travel agency, both of which sell tickets for airlines, sometimes at a substantial discount. Your best deals are likely to be for overseas travel during busy seasons when few sale fares are available. The downside is you may not earn frequent flier miles on your trip, if your flight is cancelled the airline may not be required to put you on another flight, and refunds may be nonexistent if you cannot travel. Be careful when using one of these agencies: pay with your credit card, if possible, and make sure you understand all restrictions and refund policies. You can usually buy consolidator tickets through your local travel agency, which may add a measure of comfort (but no better terms).

You may consider using frequent flier miles for part or all of your travel. Miles are estimated to be worth about two cents per mile, so compare the cost of cashing in your miles with buying a discount ticket. If you stay at a hotel or rent a car, be sure to ask whether you can earn frequent flier miles, and consider using miles for hotel stays or other types of awards.

Cruising there...

If you dream of a cruise, book early to get the best rates and cabin within your price range. Work with a travel agent who specializes in cruises to make sure you're getting the best deal possible. Alternatively, some discount travel clubs (see our list) may offer rebates or specials on cruises. While cruises are all-inclusive, you will need to budget for drinks, side trips, tips and souvenirs.

Staying there...

Hotels will often quote their highest rate if you call their toll-free reservation numbers. To get a better deal, call the hotel where you plan to stay directly, and ask about specials or discounts. Members of travel clubs like AAA or Traveler's Advantage can often get discounts, so it may be worthwhile to join one of these organizations. (See our listing, below).

Suite hotels include cooking facilities, which can be a real money saver, even if you just make your own breakfasts and lunches. If you're planning on feeding the family, check to find out whether you'll actually have a stove and refrigerator, or just a microwave oven and a mini-fridge.

Camping, whether in an RV, camper, or a tent, can make for an inexpensive and adventurous vacation. National and state parks may also rent out clean and comfortable cabins for lodging, at nice rates. (Visit www.nationalparks.org for a list of national parks, or www.mindspring.com/~wxrnot/parks.html for a list of state parks.) Some universities rent out dorm rooms during holidays or the summer, and the prices can be very low. You may have to state an educational purpose for staying there, but the rules are usually lenient.

Enjoying it...

If you'll be traveling overseas, use your credit cards when possible for a good exchange rate. Major credit card companies exchange purchases at wholesale rates, which are better than you can get on your own. And before you leave, ask your card issuer if it charges a 1% conversion fee for overseas purchases. Some do, some don't. Just make sure you pay your bill in full when it arrives so interest charges won't blow your budget!

If you rent a car at your destination, use a credit card that offers free Collision Damage Waiver (CDW) coverage to avoid paying for rental car insurance. This benefit alone can save you $10 or more a day! (Keep in mind that CDW is not accepted in all countries. Check with your travel agent and/or the company from which you will be renting in advance.) If you don't have a credit card that offers such coverage, call your own car insurer and find out what is covered when you rent a car. Your own insurance will often suffice, at least for rentals in the United States.

Before automatically renting a car at the airport, check the prices at off-airport locations. These can sometimes be cheaper, and the savings may outweigh the cost of a taxi to the rental agency.

Senior Specials...

Seniors can enjoy discounts on airfares, lodging, meals, as well as entertainment and activities at their destinations. Almost all major airlines offer both senior coupons (which are purchased in advance) as well as discounts on flights booked by seniors. Many hotels also offer discount programs for senior travelers, and most do not charge an annual fee. For just $8 you can join the American Association of Retired Persons (AARP) once you turn 50, and you'll get access to many discount services. (1-800-424-3410; www.aarp.org)

And Deals for Youth and Students...

Students and children are sometimes eligible for discounts on airfares, and they may get free lodging or meals if they are young and are accompanied by an adult. Still, traveling with a family can add up, so find out ahead of time if any special discounts are available.

Travel Resources

- ConsumerWorld is the most comprehensive site for information on discount travel. Visit www.consumerworld.org for information on airlines, cruises, places to stay, discount travel agencies, and to sign up for regular notices of last-minute airfare specials.

- Expedia is a popular website for vacation planning: expedia.msn.com.

- Fodors, the travel guide folks, also offers a variety of travel resources: www.fodors.com.

- Travel Now is best known for its listing of 20,000 hotels in 5,000 cities in 140 countries: www.travelnow.com.

- Students and adventurous others can get travel specials and tips at www.budgettravel.com.

Travel Clubs

- Costco Travel (no separate membership fee, but requires Costco membership): 1-800-800-8505; www.costcotravel.com

- Sam's Travel Club (similar to Costco): 1-800-955-7267

- Traveler's Advantage ($59.95): 1-800-548-1116; www.travelersadvantage.com

Half-price Hotel Programs

These programs offer discounts on hotels, meals, car rentals, cruises, etc. There may be restrictions on booking discount hotel rooms, and their "half-price" rate may not actually be half of the cheapest rate. But generally, these programs can save you money, especially if you plan ahead. Alternatives: Your travel agent may be able to get you a discounted rate competitive with one of these programs, and if you are a member of AAA or AARP (for seniors) you're likely to be eligible for discounts through them.

- Entertainment Publications ($64.95): 1-800-445-4137; www.entertainmentbooks.com
- Encore ($59.95): 1-800-444-9800; www.emitravel.com
- ITC-50 ($52): 1-800-987-6216
- Hotel Reservations Network (no fee): 1-800-964-6835; www.180096hotel.com

CHAPTER 34

How to Start Your Own Successful Business With Little Money

Tired of the 9 to 5 grind? Considering going into business for yourself? You're not alone. Millions of people have a similar dream. A few brave ones take the next step. Unfortunately, for many, the dream can turn into a nightmare quickly. The U.S. Small Business Administration statistics show that well over half of all new small businesses fail. Bankruptcy professionals can tell you that a disproportionate amount of the debt wiped out in personal bankruptcy cases comes from personal liability on small business debt. These numbers aren't meant to stop you from pursuing your dream. They are meant as a warning—know the risk up front so you take steps to minimize future financial ruin.

One fundamental question a small business person getting started must answer is "Where will I get the money to finance my business?". This chapter suggests some options and the risks involved with each.

First Things First

Before you consider the sources of funds, heed this warning: **Don't make the common mistake of pouring too much money into your business at the outset.** Take time to figure out if your business will be viable. Spending borrowed money on an untested business idea can lead to disaster. Most small businesses don't require a great deal of cash or credit up front. Start small. Funds will become available if you succeed. If you don't, you can move on, debt free.

"At the present growth rate, we should reach $1 in sales any day now."

Your Current Salary

"Don't give up your day job." That advice is commonly given by nervous parents to their children who decide to become artists or writers. It applies to many entrepreneurs who are just beginning. Start small and you may be able to stay afloat for many months by continuing your full-time job or cutting back to part-time. The steady source of income can reduce your need for turning to others for start-up funds and can help keep you solvent if the business fails.

Personal Savings

Putting your own money into your business is the simplest way to get started. You avoid entanglements with others, keep your business affairs private and avoid taking on repayment obligations. The money may come from savings or from a lump sum that comes once, such as an inheritance or severance package from a job you've just left. If you've sold your house and have bought a less expensive one or will rent, you should have some money to invest in your business.

Retirement Savings

If you have a retirement savings plan where you work, you may be able to borrow some of that money. Check the plan language to see if loans are allowed for business purposes. If so, you should be able to borrow up to one-half of what you have in the plan, but no more than $50,000. Also check the maximum term allowed for a loan (typically five years), the interest rate and the loan fees. You will have to pay interest on the money you borrow from your plan, but that's not all bad. Because you are borrowing from yourself, the interest goes back to you.

If you've reached the age of 59 1/2, you can simply take rather than borrow money from the tax-deferred plan, without paying a penalty. Before that age, however, you would owe a substantial penalty for early withdrawal and you would owe taxes on the amount withdrawn.

Equity in Your Home

If you own a home, you may be able to tap into a portion of the equity to raise cash. Equity is the difference between what the home is worth and how much you owe on it. For example, if your house is worth $300,000 and you owe your mortgage lender $140,000, your equity is $160,000.

One way to get to the equity is to get a new mortgage to pay off the existing one, which will leave you with cash for your business. On that $300,000 home, you obtained a new mortgage for $240,000-80% of the home's current value. You'll have $80,000 to invest in your business after the mortgage is paid off.

Another approach is to apply for a line of credit based on your home equity. The bank will have a second mortgage on your home. Typically, the bank will give you a checkbook which you can use to write checks against the line of credit. Your monthly payment will depend on how much of the credit line you've used.

Whichever method you choose, realize that you are putting your home at risk if you don't repay the loan. Don't borrow more than you absolutely need. And figure out how you'll make the mortgage payments if your business starts out slowly or fails. Consider a loan with a long repayment window—which means lower monthly payments. If your business does well, you can repay it sooner.

The Seller of the Business

If you will buy an existing business, try negotiating with the seller for favorable payment terms. This will reduce the amount of cash you have to come up with. First, try to keep the down payment low. Second, ask the seller to agree to below-market interest rates or even no interest for the first year or two. Third, try for an extended payment term over many years.

Friends and Relatives

Those close to you will often lend you money or invest in your business. By borrowing money from people you know, you may be charged a relatively low interest rate, may be able to delay paying back money until you get yourself established and may be given flexibility if you get into a jam.

But borrowing money from relatives and friends can have a big downside. If your business does poorly and those close to you lose money, you'll damage a personal relationship. So in dealing with friends and relatives, be extra careful to not only clearly establish the terms of the deal and put it in writing, but also make an extra effort to explain the risks.

Banks and the Small Business Administration

Banks are in the money business, so it's natural to look to them for start-up funds. But banks are reluctant to lend anything substantial until a business has established a record of profitability.

There is an exception, however. If you present a loan guaranteed by the U.S. Small Business Administration (SBA), a bank may respond more favorably. The SBA is more likely to guarantee a loan for someone expanding a successful business than for someone just starting out, but it never hurts to talk with the SBA about your new business.

Credit Cards

You can use your credit cards to help finance your business. Plastic can quickly get you a computer and fax machine—and probably other business equipment and furniture as well. And for expenses such as rent, phone bills or money to pay employees, you can usually get a cash advance.

Credit cards are a convenient way to arrange for short-term financing because they're so easy to use. Over the long haul, however, they're a disaster—the interest charges on new purchases average about 19% per year and on cash advances is as high as 25% per year. You're not likely to succeed in business by incurring debt at those rates.

Buying on Credit

The companies from which you're buying goods or services may let you buy on credit—not requiring payment for 30 or 60 days—to get your business. If they won't extend you credit, they may let you spread payments over several months with no interest charges, as long as you pay each installment on time. Even if they do charge interest, it will no doubt be substantially less than what your credit card issuer charges.

Typically, the best credit terms go to established businesses; new businesses often must pay up front. But credit decisions can be subjective. You may be able to convince the seller that your new business deserves special consideration. Especially if you need starting inventory, call suppliers and ask for help. Have a copy of your credit history and business plan. If you're persuasive, you may be able to get a fair amount of your inventory on favorable terms.

Leasing

If you need equipment, consider leasing it. While leasing doesn't put money directly in your hands, it does reduce the amount of cash you'd have to come up with if you were to buy equipment. In considering leases, look for ones that include an option to buy the equipment when the lease period is over, as long as the purchase price is reasonable. Over the long term, leasing usually costs more than buying, but if the cash flow from your business will be tight for a few years, leasing can be an effective way to get the equipment you need now.

Equity Investors

Equity investors buy a piece of your business. They are co-owners and share the fortunes and misfortunes. Generally, if your business does badly or flops, you're under no obligation to pay them back their money.

Some equity investors insist on a guarantee of some return on their investment, even if the business does poorly. Unless you're desperate for the cash, avoid an investor who wants a guarantee. It's simply too risky a proposition for someone starting a small business.

Corporate shares, limited partnership interests and in some states, an interest in a limited liability company, are legally considered to be securities, which are regulated by federal and state law. This means that before selling an investor an interest in your business, you'll need to learn more about the requirements of the securities laws.

CHAPTER 35

Identity Theft: How to Protect Yourself and What to Do if You Are a Victim

Think your money and peace-of-mind are safe from thieves? Think again. You may have a handle on your cash, but how careful are you with your identifying information? Identity theft is one of the fastest growing types of robbery today. In 1997, identity theft cost consumers and financial institutions $745 million. Approximately 40,000 people have their identities stolen each year.

Identity theft occurs when a thief gets your identifying information and poses as you to run up your existing credit cards, open new credit cards and bank accounts, drain bank accounts, apply for jobs and housing, get loans, open utilities and long distance phone accounts, get false identities, and write false checks. Identity thieves can even commit crimes then give their fake identity (your name) to police when they are arrested.

Unfortunately, the way that most people find out that their identity has been stolen is by getting a collection call from an agency they never worked with, or by being denied a loan because of a bad credit rating, when they have always paid their bills on time. Although the victim of identity theft may not be responsible for the actual debt, he or she may be left with a bad credit report that can takes years to correct. This bad credit report affects a consumer in every facet of his life—his ability to get loans, mortgages, bank accounts, rent apartments—and maybe even destroys job chances. Victims spend hundreds of hours and thousands of dollars straightening out their credit records.

Fortunately, Congress has listened to the victims of identity theft and in October 1998, enacted the Identity Theft and Assumption Deterrence Act, which gives victims a weapon against identity thieves and gives victims a single place where they can file a complaint and get consumer information. The Identity Theft and Assumption Deterrence Act criminalizes fraud in the connection with theft and misuse of personal identifying information. Anyone who steals another person's identity and gains $1,000 within one year from misusing that identity, is subject to a fine and imprisonment of up to 20 years.

Some states have also criminalized identity theft. Check your consumer protection or consumer affairs office to see if your state has such a law, and how it can help you.

How Does a Thief Get My Identity Information?

It is very easy for a thief to get important information from you. A thief can get information from you by:

- Sifting through your mail and stealing your bills, credit card applications, pre-approved cards, bank or credit card statements, or credit cards.

- Looking through your trash for credit or debit card slips, checks, credit card applications, or other documents with identifying information.

- Stealing your wallet.

- A merchant's employee stealing your identification information from a check or credit card slip.

- Filling out a change of address card to divert your mail to the thief's address.

- Relatives, roommates, friends, household workers, ex-spouses using your identity without your authority.

- Obtaining a copy of your credit report by pretending to be someone with a "legitimate business purpose" to the information under the Fair Credit Reporting Act.

- Watching you punch in your Personal Identification Number ("PIN") at Automated Teller Machines ("ATM") or public telephones.

The personal information that thieves want and that you should be very careful to protect includes: your Social Security Number, your mother's maiden name, your passwords and PINs for debit and long distance telephone cards, credit card numbers, old and current addresses, and your birth date.

How Can I Prevent Identity Thieves From Getting My Information?

Identity theft is prevalent because it is so easy to do and so hard to detect. But you can be pro-active to make it harder for thieves to get your personal information and easier for you to detect fraudulent activity. Taking pro-active steps is especially important because it is so difficult to erase the false information from all your identifying documents, such as your credit report. The following steps will help you police your information and reduce the overall information on you:

- Pay attention to your billing cycles and contact creditors if bills do not arrive on time. Also, know when new or reissued credit cards will be coming in the mail.

- Leave all unnecessary documents at home, including excess credit cards or identification (such as your birth certificate or passport).

- Keep documents with personal information, like canceled checks, in a safe place and shred them when you don't need them anymore. Documents that you should shred include credit card receipts, copies of credit applications, insurance forms, bank checks and statements, and old credit or debit/ATM cards.

- Document all important creditor information—contact information, account numbers, expiration dates, and any other relevant information—and keep it in a safe place in your home.

- Don't dispose of identifying information, like an ATM, debit card, or credit card slip, in a public trash can. Even some store receipts have your credit card information on them. Examine all receipts before publicly discarding.

- Cancel all unused credit card accounts so that an identity thief cannot get these account numbers from your credit report.

- Opt out of pre-approved offers of credit by removing your name from the marketing lists of the three major credit bureaus. Write to the following credit bureaus and tell them that you want to opt out of pre-approved offers of credit, and request that they remove your name from their marketing lists:

Equifax Options
P.O. Box 740123
Atlanta, GA 30374-0123
888-567-8688

Trans Union
P.O. Box 97328
Jackson, MS 39238
800-680-7293

Experian
P.O. Box 919
Allen, TX 75013
800-353-0809

- Sign up for the Direct Marketing Association's Mail and Telephone Preference Services. Write to the following addresses and ask to be added to "name deletion lists" to stop mail and telemarketing.

  Mail Preference Service
  P.O. Box 9008
  Farmingdale, NY 11735

  Telephone Preference Service
  P.O. Box 9014
  Farmingdale, NY 11735

- Consider having your name and address removed from the phone book and directories. Contact your local telephone company to find out how to get an unlisted telephone number.

- Get a Post Office Box or get a locked mailbox to deter thieves from stealing your mail.

- Pick up newly ordered checks at the bank to avoid having blank checks in your mailbox.

- Be sure to mail all paid bills at the post office or use a public mailbox.

- Be smart when giving personal information over the phone. If you have any doubts about the person asking the information, hang up and initiate the call yourself.

- Check your credit report annually. You can get a consolidated report from all three major credit bureaus through DCA's website at www.GetOutOfDebt.org. Complete the investigation form if you find any inaccuracies that you want to dispute.

- Be smart when picking a Personal Identification Number ("PIN") or password. Thieves assume you'll use a number that is easy to remember, like the last four digits of your Social Security Number or your birth date. Don't have your PIN written and placed next to your card.

- Make sure no one can see you punch in your PIN or password at the ATM or merchant, or your telephone card number at a public telephone.

- Be protective of your Social Security Number ("SSN"). If someone asks for it, such as when you write a check, see if you can provide another number. There are some forms where it is necessary, such as your tax forms.

What Should I Do if My Identity Is Stolen?

If your identity is stolen, you have to take steps first to ensure that the thief can no longer pose as you, and then to restore your credit history and good name. Fortunately, you may not be responsible for debt that a thief incurs using your name. (If an identity thief runs up credit cards in your name, and you notify your creditors, the most that you will be responsible for is $50. Under federal law, you are liable for more with debit cards, but the industry generally treats debit cards like credit cards. (See Chapter 13, "Credit Card or Debit Card, the Great Debate.") If your identity has been stolen, you should do the following IMMEDIATELY:

- Notify creditors by phone as soon as you discover the theft, ask for the fraud department, and have them close all your accounts. Follow up with a certified letter, return receipt requested, confirming your telephone call.

- Call the Fraud Divisions of the major credit bureaus to ask that a "fraud alert" be placed in your file.

    Experian   888-397-3742 (www.experian.com)

    Trans Union   800-680-7289 (www.tuc.com)

    Equifax   800-525-6285 (www.equifax.com)

    Add a "victim's statement" explaining that your identity was stolen. This statement may be placed in your file for a limited period of time, so be sure to renew it if necessary.

- Call the local police and report the fraud. Some banks or credit card companies may require you to show a police report to verify the crime.

- Call your bank/credit union and cancel old account numbers, PINs, and your ATM and debit cards, and get new ones. You should report false checks/bank accounts to the following check guarantee companies so that they will flag your file and ensure counterfeit checks will be refused:

    TeleCheck   800-710-9898

    National Processing Company (NPC)   800-526-5380

    Equifax   800-437-5120

- If you suspect that someone is using your driver's license number, call the Department of Motor Vehicles ("DMV"). The DMV can tell you if it issued another license in your name. If this is the case, get a new number and ask the DMV to investigate the identity theft. Some DMVs allow you to block your information from being released.

- Call all utilities (electrical, gas, water, local telephone, long distance telephone, and cable TV) and let them know that other services may have been fraudulently requested in your name. You may need to change account and telephone numbers.

- If your Social Security Number was used fraudulently, report the problem to the Social Security Administration's Fraud Hotline 800-269-0271. In extreme cases of fraud, you may be able to get a new SSN. At the same time, don't impulsively change your SSN as it can put burdens on you later.

- Mail fraud victims should report the fraud to their local Postal Inspection Service Office.

- An identity thief may order a passport in your name. Send a certified letter, return receipt requested to the passport office to let it know someone may pose as you to order a new passport in your name.

These steps may seem drastic, but you must be careful—don't think you're safe because you canceled your credit card and placed a stop on your checking account. Once identity thieves have your identification information, they can open new bank, credit card, utility and other accounts and lines of credit under your name.

You should keep a log of everything you do to correct the identity theft. Write down all telephone conversations in detail—date and time, name of person with whom you speak, telephone numbers, and the substance of the conversation. Send all letters by certified mail, return receipt requested. Keep copies of all letters and documents.

Under the new law, the Identity Theft and Assumption Deterrence Act of 1998, you will also notify the Federal Trade Commission (FTC) of any identity theft, which will keep a database of all complaints. The FTC is still formulating how it will handle these calls, and it has indicated that it will establish a toll-free telephone line where you will report identity theft and receive consumer information, and get referrals to the other appropriate organizations that you should contact.

Index

401(k) 31, 190
403(b) 31

A

AAA *see American Automobile Association*
AARP *see American Association of Retired Persons*
Alimony 117, 128
American Association of Retired Persons 197, 198
American Automobile Association 193, 196, 198
American Express 34, 63
ATM 65, 66, 86, 155, 206, 207, 208
Attachment of personal property 136
  Sheriff's sale 136
Automated Teller Machines *see ATM*
Automatic stay 114, 115

B

Back-to-school 175-178
Balloon payment 84
Bankruptcy 3, 83, 103, 114, 115-119, 121
  Automobiles, and 117-118
  Automatic stay 114, 115
  Business, and 199
  Chapter 13 114, 115, 118-119
  Chapter 7 114, 115-118
  Effects of 3, 53, 119
  Exempt property 117-118
  Fraud, and 116, 117
  Housing, and 118
  Liquidation 115
  Nondischargeable debts 117
  Nonexempt property 117
  Previous bankruptcy 116
  Public benefits, and 118
  Reorganization 115 *see also Chapter 13*
  Straight 115
  Student loans, and 11
  Taxes, and 117
Bankruptcy trustee 115
Banks 42, 203, 205
  Savings accounts 4-5, 9, 190
  Statements 155, 205
Beacon 51
Better Business Bureau 112, 146
Business, starting your own 199-204
Buy now, pay later 171, 179

C

Campgrounds 144-146

Cars 73-102, 184-185
　Balloon payment 84
　Bankruptcy, and 117-118
　Buying 75, 77-78, 79, 83-87
　Default 89, 94-95
　Deficiency 92, 101-102
　Extension 89
　Financing, alternative 85
　Financing, dealer's 84-85
　Insurance, prepaid 102
　Leasing *see Leases*
　Pink slip 90
　Rental 63-64, 196
　Security agreement 93
Cash advance *see Credit cards*
CDW 64, 196
Chapter 13 Bankruptcy *see Bankruptcy*
Chapter 7 Bankruptcy *see Bankruptcy*
Charge-off *see Credit, Write-off*
Checks/Checking 34, 153-158, 205
　Accounts 34
　Balancing checkbook 155
　Bounced checks 153-156
　　Fees 153-154
　Clearing policy 154
　Elements of a good check 157-158
　Guarantee companies 209
　Receiving bad check 156
　Verification companies 154
　Writing tips 154
Child support 147-151
　Amount 147
　Bankruptcy, and 117, 149
　Changing amount 148
　Enforcement of 149, 150, 151
　Genetic testing 149
　Increasing amount 148
　Moving 150
　Paternity 149
　Reducing amount 148
　Remarriage 148
　Right to support 150
　State help 149
　Termination 151
　Visitation 148

Children 175-178
Collateral 5, 27, 94
Collection agency 165 *see also Debt collectors*
College, and credit cards 179-181
Collision Damage Waiver *see CDW*
Commingled accounts 38
Community property 128
Complaints, court 133, 134
　Answering 134
Consumer Affairs office/agency 21, 68, 94, 142, 146
Consumer Credit Reporting Reform Act 45
Consumer Federation of America 183
Consumer Leasing Act 91
Consumer Protection office/agency *see Consumer Affairs office*
Contracts 5, 139-146
　Acceleration clause 95
　Canceling 141, 142, 143, 146, 168
　Cooling-off period 141, 143
　Costs 143
　Extension 89
　Installment contracts 168-169
　Refund 139, 141
　Rescission rights 28
Conversion fees 63, 196
Cosign 1, 42, 110, 116, 124, 165
Costco Travel 197
Court, small claims 133, 134
Credit 1, 23, 57-59, 61-64, 171-173, 203-204 *see also Loans*
　Billing errors 26-27, 67
　Closed-end credit 25
　College, and 179-181
　History 51, 52, 72
　References 34
　Write off 29-30
Credit bureaus 45, 136 *see also Equifax, Experian, and Trans Union*
Credit cards 3, 42, 61-64, 123-124, 179-182, 188-189, 196, 203 *see also Credit*

Annual fees 24
Annual percentage rate 24
Authorized user 42
Applications 3, 33
Balances 123-124
Bill statements 24, 26
Billing cycles 26, 207
Billing errors 67, 71
Cash advances 2, 5
Closed accounts 47, 56, 130, 131
   Closed by consumer 39, 47, 56, 123-124, 130
Dispute with merchant 62, 67-68, 71
Grace period 25, 71
Incentives 58, 66
Interest rates 3, 5, 57, 180
Late fees 66
Limit 65
Lost 63 see also Credit cards, Stolen
Minimum monthly payments 4, 65
Preapproved credit cards 49-50, 58, 207
Rating 67 see also Credit reports
Secured cards 2, 42, 67
Stolen 63, 68, 72, 205-210
Students and credit cards 179-181
Surfing 56
Terms 24-25
Theft see Stolen
Transaction fees 24-25
Travel, with 63, 193-198
User fees 24-25
Credit record 189 see also Credit reports
Credit repair 37-44
   Clinics 43-44
Credit reports 2, 37-42, 181, 206, 208
   100-word statement 2, 40, 131
   Disclosures, required 47-48
   Dispute procedure 38-40, 45-47, 55-56
   Free reports 48, 59
   Mistakes 38-40, 45-47, 55-56
   Negative information 2, 49, 53, 83, 103, 189
   Positive information 40-41
   Reporting agencies 45 see also Credit bureaus
   Victim's statement 209
Credit scoring 33-35, 51-56, 59
   Application scores 51
   Fair Isaac Company 51-56
   FICO see Fair Isaac Company
   Four Reason Codes 53-54
   Improving your score 55-56
Cutting expenses 122-123

D

Damages, in lawsuit 133
Debit cards 65-72, 209
   Billing errors 67, 71
   Credit history, and 72
   Disputes with merchant 67-68, 71
   Fees 66, 71
   Floating period 65-66, 71
   Theft protection 68, 72
   Unauthorized withdrawals 68, 72
Debt
   Consolidation 59
   Military career, and your 159
   Nondischargeable 117
Debt collectors 17-21, 160-162
   Collection accounts 35
   Communications with third parties 20
   Disclosures, required 18
   Fair Debt Collections Practices Act 17, 19, 20, 21, 160-162
   Harrassment 17-21
   Identification 18
   Insults 19
   IRS, and 29-31
   Military and 160-166
   Stopping calls 20-21
   Threats 18, 30
   Violation of the law 21
Debt Counselors of America 4, 59, 67, 119, 121, 162, 179, 180, 190, 194

Debt Eliminator 4, 59
Default 11, 15-16, 83, 94-95, 103
Default judgment 134, 165-166
Deferment 13-15, 186 see also Student loans
Deficiency 90, 101
Delinquency see Late payments
Department of Agriculture 184
Department of Education 15, 16, 186
  Debt Collection Services office 15
Department of Motor Vehicles see DMV
Department of Real Estate 112
Direct Loan Program 12, 13 see also Student loans
Direct Marketing Association 208
Directory of Designated Low-Income Schools for Teacher Cancellation Benefits 186
Discounts 176, 193-197
  Dollar stores 176
  Hotels 198
  Office supplies 176
  Travel, and 193-197
Discover 34
Disposible income, bankruptcy 119
Divorce 41, 127-131
  Bankruptcy, and 117
  Community property, and 128
  Debts, and 129-130
  Property, and 127-129
DMV 209

E

Edelman, Ric 190
Education Resources Institute 179
EIN see Employer Identification Number
EMPIRICA 51
Employer Identification Number (EIN) 43
Employment 34, 40, 48, 53, 83
  Lay-offs 184
Encore 198

Entertainment Publications 198
Entrepreneurs 199-204
Equifax 40, 50, 51, 181, 205, 207, 209
Equitable disposition 128, 168
  Divorce, and 128
  Military, and 168
Everybody's Guide to Small Claims Court 133
Eviction 163, 167-168
Ex-spouses 41, 127-131
Exchange rate 196
Expedia 197
Experian 40, 50, 51, 181, 208, 209

F

Fair Credit Billing Act 26, 62, 67
Fair Credit Reporting Act 43, 45-50
Fair Debt Collection Practices Act 17, 19, 20, 21, 160, 161
Fair Isaac Company see Credit scoring
Fannie Mae 110, 111, 113
FBI 156
Federal Housing Administration 113
Federal Reserve Bank of Boston 154, 157, 158
Federal Reserve Board 28, 156, 157
Federal Reserve number 156, 157
Federal Student Aid Information Center 15
Federal Trade Commission 21, 49, 146, 210
Fodors 197
Forbearance 15, 186, 187 see also Student loans
Foreclosure 83, 109-110, 163, 165, 168
  Deed in lieu of 113-114
  Judicial 109
  Non-judicial 109
  Pre-foreclosure investors 112
  Quit-claim deed 113
  Strict foreclosure see Repossession
Fraud

Debts from 117
  Identity theft, and 206
Freddie Mac 110, 111, 113
Frequent flier miles 195
FTC *see Federal Trade Commission*

G

Gap insurance 79
Garnishment 4, 135-136, 165
  of bank accounts 136
  of wages 4, 135-136, 165
Graduates 183-190
Guaranteed account 42
Guarantors 42, 124, 165

H

Health clubs 139-142
  Cancellation 141
  Getting out of 142
High-risk investments 125
Holidays 171-174
  Credit strategies for 171-173
  Entertaining during 174
  Gifts 173-174, 178
Home equity loan *see Loans*
Hotel Reservations Network 198
Housing 27-28, 109-114
  Bankruptcy, and 118
  Buying 103-107
  Financing, seller 106-107
  Graduates, and 184, 187-188
  Military, and 167-168
  Regulation Z, and 27-28

I

Identity theft 205-210
  Prevention 205
Identity Theft and Assumption Deterrence Act 205, 206, 208, 210
Inheritance 128, 201
Initiation fees 141
Inquiries 35, 38, 48-49, 56

Insolvent (IRS) 30, 114
Institute for Higher Education Policy 179
Insurance 79, 123, 169
  Gap 79
  Medical 123
  Military, and 169
  Pre-paid premiums 102
  Purchase Mortgage Insurance *see PMI*
Internal Revenue Service *see IRS*
Internet-travel sites 197-198
Investing 4-5, 125, 183-184, 189-190, 204
IRA 31
  Roth IRA 190
IRS 29-31, 112, 167 *see also Taxes*
  Form 1099 29-31, 114
  Form 1099-A 29-31
  Form 1099-C 29-31
  Settlement and 29-31
ITC-50 198

J

Joint property 125, 128
Judgment 35, 38, 39, 56, 83, 103, 117
  Creditor 135, 136
  Default 134, 165-166
  Satisfaction of 136
Judicial sale of car 99 *see also Repossession*

K

Keogh plan 31

L

Late payments 34, 38, 52, 54, 83, 103
Lawsuits 133-137, 165-167
  Filing 133-134
Leases, automobile 73-81, 86-87
  Acquisition fee 75, 87
  Adjusted capitalized cost 73
  Assumability 81

Closed-end 86
Deferment 81
Depreciation, monthly 74
Excess mileage 86
Extension 81
Gap insurance 79, 87
Getting out of 90
Inception fees 87
Lease rate, monthly 74
Money factor 74
Negotiated vehicle price 73
Net cap cost 73
Open-end 86
Residual value 73, 80
Security deposit 75, 87
Substitution 81
Termination 79, 81-87, 91
  Early 79, 81, 87
Trade in 79
Warranty 80, 87
Wear and tear 86
Leasing, equipment for business 204
Leonard, Robin 15, 153
Lien 35, 38, 56, 83, 103, 165
Limited liability company 204
Limited partnership 204
Liquidation 114, 115 *see also Bankruptcy*
Loan-to-value ratio 75
Loans 5, 43, 203 *see also Credit*
  Approving 3
  Automobile *see Cars*
  Conventional 104
  Consolidation of 5, 59
  Defaulting on 11, 83, 94-95, 103
  Home equity 2, 5 *see also Mortgages*
    Business, and 201-202
  Military, and 168
  Prequalification 104
  Student *see Student loans*

M

Mail and Telephone Preference Services 208
Mail fraud 210
Maintenance 147 *see also Child support and Alimony*
Marital property 127-129
Marriage and credit 41
MasterCard 34, 63, 65, 68
MasterMoney 65
Medical insurance 123
Merchants
  Local 43
  Dispute with 62, 67-68, 71
Military 14, 159-170
  Active duty 163
  Debt, and 159-162
  Housing 167
  Interest rates, and 163, 169
  Installment contracts, and 168-169
  Insurance, and 169
  Just financial obligations 159
  Letters of Indebtedness 160
  Relocation 159
  Repossession, and 97
  Student loans, and 14
  Taxes 169
Money gobblers 184, 198-197
Mortgages 103-114
  A loans 105
  B loans 105
  Brokers, mortgage 111
  Buydown 107
  C loans 105
  D loans 105
  Deed of trust 110
  PMI *see Private Mortgage Insurance*
  Prequalified 104
  Private Mortgage Insurance (PMI) 111
  Traditional 110

N

National Automobile Dealers Association (NADA) 101
National Consumers League 65
National Processing Company (NPC) 209
NationsBank 183
Native Americans, and repossession 97

O

On-Track 9, 37, 59, 121, 173
One-Pay 119
Overdraft protection, in checking 154
Overpayment 25-16

P

Passport 207, 210
Passwords 65, 206, 208
Perkins loans 15 *see also Student loans*
Personal Identification Number 65, 70, 72, 206, 208
Petition 133 *see also Complaint*
PIN *see Personal Identification Number*
Pleadings 134
PMI *see Purchase Mortgage Insurance*
Post-dated checks 154
Postal Inspection Service Office 210
Pre-approved credit offers 49, 207
  Opting out 207-208
  Prescreening block 50
Prequalification letter 104
Private Mortgage Insurance 111
Process server 134
Promissory notes 128

Q

Quill 176
Quitclaim deed 113

R

Redemption 92, 99 *see also Repossession*
Regulation Z 23-28 *see also Truth in Lending Act*
  Dispute procedure 26-27
  Homeowners, and 27-28
  Required disclosures 24-25
  Rescission rights 28
Reinstatement of contract 92, 98 *see also repossession*
Rent 74, 124, 204
Repossession 83, 89, 91, 93-102
  Acceleration 95, 102
  Breach of peace 97-98
  Consent to 96
  Constructive strict foreclosure 99
  Delay of sale 99, 101
  Disposition of vehicle 98-100
  Military, and 97, 163, 165, 168
  Native Americans 97
  Notice of acceleration 96
  Notice of sale 100
  Recondition 101
  Redemption of car 92, 99
  Reinstatement of contract 92, 98
  Repo man 92
  Right to cure 95, 96
  Sale 92, 99-101
    Creditor sale 100-101
    Judicial 99
    Notice of 100
  Security agreement 93, 94
  Self-help repossession 96-98
  Strict forclosure 99, 101
  Voluntary 90
Retirement 4-5, 201
Right to cure default 95, 96 *see repossession*
Risk scoring *see credit scoring*
Roommates 187-188, 206

S

Sallie Mae 184
Sam's Travel Club 197
Satisfaction of judgment 136
Savings accounts *see Banks*
SBA *see Small Business Administration*
School 175-178
Secondarily liable, and the military 165
Secured cards 2, 42, 67
Security deposit for automobiles 75, 87
Self-help repossession 96-98
Service of process 134
Settlement of debts 29-31
Short sale 112-113, 114
Shredding documents 207
Small Business Administration (SBA) 199, 203
Small claims court 133, 134
Social Security Administration's Fraud Hotline 210
Social Security Number (SSN) 38, 43, 206, 208, 210
Soldiers' and Sailors' Civil Relief Act 97, 159, 162, 163-170
Spending plan 8-9, 37-38, 121-122, 184 *see also On-Track*
Statement of Claim *see Complaint*
Statute of limitations, and military 167
Stay of proceedings
  Automatic, in bankruptcy 114, 115
  Military, and 166-167, 168
Stocks 4-5
Strict foreclosure *see Repossession*
Student loans 11-16, 117, 185-187
  Cancelling 13-15
  Consolidation 13
  Department of Education 15, 16, 186
  Default 15-16
  Deferment 13-15, 186
  Disability, and 14
  Direct Loan Program 12, 13
  Extended Repayment Plan 12, 185
  Federal 12, 13, 15
  Forbearance 15, 186, 187
  Graduated Repayment Plan 11-12, 185-186
  Income Contingent Repayment Plan 12, 186
  Income Sensitive Repayment Plan 12
  Military, and 14
  Perkins loan 15
  Postponing payments 13-15, 186
  Reasonable and Affordable Repayment Plan 15-16
  Standard Repayment Plan 11, 185
  Trade school 15
Students 175-182
Summons 134
Surety, in the military 165

T

Taxes 29-31, 112 *see also IRS*
  Bankruptcy, and 117
  Deductions 5
  Short Sale, and 114
  State taxes, and military 169
TeleCheck 209
Telephone Preference Service 208
Timeshares 142-144
  Getting out of 143
Trade-in, cars 79
Trade schools 15
Trans Union 40, 50-51, 181, 207, 209
Travel 63-64, 193-197
  Consolidators 195
  Hotels 198
  Internet sites 197-198
  Travel Advantages 63
  Travel clubs 144-146, 197
  Travel Now 197
  Traveler's Advantage 196, 197
Truth About Money, The 190
Truth in Lending Act 23-28, 63 *see also Regulation Z*
TRW/FICO 51

U

Unfair and Deceptive Acts and Practices 144
Utilities 184, 188, 205, 209-210

V

Vacation 193-197 *see also Travel*
Variable rate 25
Victim's statement 209
Virginia Tech 160
Visa 34, 63, 65, 68

W

Wage garnishment 4, 135, 165
Warner, Ralph 133
Warranty 80, 87
  Manufacturer's 80
Writ of attachment 136
Writ of garnishment 135 *see also Garnishment and Wage garnishment*
Work at home 2

Websites mentioned throughout our book

www.180096hotel.com 198
www.aarp.org 197
www.bankrate.com 58
www.budgettravel.com 197
www.cardtrak.com 58, 62
www.consumer-action.com 62
www.consumerworld.org 197
www.costcotravel.com 197
www.credit.com 47
www.emitravel.com 198
www.entertainmentbooks.com 198
www.equifax.com 181
www.experian.com 181
www.fodors.com 197
www.GetOutOfDebt.org
  59, 67, 121, 124, 133, 173, 180, 194
www.mindspring.com/~wxrnot/parks.html 196
www.nationalparks.org 196
www.quillcorp.com 176
www.reliable.com 176
www.transunion.com 181
www.travelersadvantage.com 197
www.travelnow.com 197

To order additional copies of this book...

Visit www.GetOutOfDebt.org
or call 1-800-680-3328.

Relax. We're here to help.

Dealing with difficult financial issues?

Whether you visit us on the web or call us on the phone, at **Debt Counselors of America**® (DCA®), you'll find solutions. We've helped more than two million consumers through our web site and counseling services, and we can help you too. Our programs include:

One-Pay® - Pay back debts, stop collection calls. One easy, lower monthly payment.

Crisis Relief Team℠ - Rapid response assistance to help you deal with potential bankruptcy, foreclosure, judgements and more...

Debt Eliminator® - Get out of debt as quickly as possible and save on interest payments.

DebtChat℠ - Talk one-on-one with a counselor in our **private** chat room.

Get Out Of Debt℠**-The Radio Show** - Listen to our weekly radio show and call-in with your questions.

Debt Counselors of America®

Helping people manage current debt responsibilities and avoid future financial problems.

www.GetOutOfDebt.org 1-800-680-3328

You've read the book.
Now speak to the authors live.

No bull.
No beating around the bush.

Callers get great advice
from the "Dastardly Duo of Debt,"
Steve Rhode and Mike Kidwell.

Visit us on the web to find out more.
www.DebtRadio.com